Tricksters and Cosmopolitans

Tricksters and Cosmopolitans

Cross-Cultural Collaborations in Asian American Literary Production

REI MAGOSAKI

Fordham University Press
NEW YORK 2016

Fordham University Press also publishes its books in a variety of electronic formats. Some content that appears in print may not be available in electronic books.

Visit us online at www.fordhampress.com.

Library of Congress Cataloging-in-Publication Data available online at catalog.loc.gov.

Printed in the United States of America

18 17 16   5 4 3 2 1

First edition

THE AMERICAN LITERATURES INITIATIVE

A book in the American Literatures Initiative (ALI), a collaborative publishing project of NYU Press, Fordham University Press, Rutgers University Press, Temple University Press, and the University of Virginia Press. The Initiative is supported by The Andrew W. Mellon Foundation. For more information, please visit www.americanliteratures.org.

Contents

Acknowledgments

I would like to thank Chapman University and Wilkinson College of Arts, Humanities, and Social Sciences for the tremendous institutional support they have given me for the research and scholarly activity related to this project, allowing me to travel to archives and present on my findings. The Japan Foundation of New York, East/West Consortium, and Play for Japan became joint sponsors, which provided the time and space necessary to complete the manuscript, and I am very grateful for the generosity of Florida Atlantic University in opening up their resources, as well as for the goodwill of its faculty members and staff during the year I spent as their scholar in residence. I am indebted to Tom Lay at Fordham University Press for reading through the draft and bringing my work to the attention of the late Helen Tartar that year. I would like to thank the anonymous readers for their strong support and detailed suggestions for revision; I benefited and learned much from their constructive criticism. It has been a pleasure and honor to work with Richard Morrison, whose enthusiasm and encouragement have meant a lot to me, and I truly appreciate the hard work of his team.

It gives me great pleasure to express my appreciation for the teachers, colleagues, and friends who helped me in different ways as I wrote this book. A huge thanks goes to Joanna Levin and Michael Wood for their time and attention in reading the entire manuscript. Rita Felski's mentorship and friendship have extended over many years, and Dale E. Peterson's presence when I needed reliable guidance has been just as important. I have been blessed to receive advice and support from Karen

Sanchez-Eppler, Alan Nadel, Jennifer Wicke, Eric Lott, Don Pease, Yunte Huang, Rei Terada, and Scott Saul; at Chapman, there was Jeanne Gunner, Richard Ruppel, Kevin O'Brien, Stephanie Takaragawa, Mildred Lewis, and Tom Zoellner. Sylvia Chong receives a special thanks for taking me under her wing and introducing me to the Association for Asian American Studies, one of the most vibrant and critically savvy intellectual communities I have known, which has nurtured my development as a scholar in important ways. It was an unexpected gift that I came to know Stephen Vincent as a friend during the process of conducting research. His sustained interest in my work fed the drive to write, as did my interactions with Lawson Inada, Maxine Hong Kingston, Hilton Obenzinger, Jessica Hagedorn, Min Jin Lee, Monique Truong, Linda E. Norton, and Christine Balance.

This book is dedicated to my parents in Tokyo, Ukeru and Noriko Magosaki, who made it possible for me to continue my pursuit of dreams across the Pacific. I would like to honor the memory of Sumiko Iba, Karen Gifford, and Don Will alongside my close friends on both sides of the Pacific whose lives are inspirational: Akiko Saito, Takayo Ando, Eri Harada, Akoya Soda, Takako Tahira, Junko Okahashi, Miki Sode, Keisuke Goda, Aki Yoshino, Masaki Nakayama, Ami Yamasaki, Mayumi Matsubara, Noriko Shimodaira, Noriko Donahue, Nubar Hovsepian, Carmichael Peters, Anna Leahy, Jan Osborn, Justine Van Meter, Sarah Hagelin, Maria Windell, Jolie Sheffer, and Penny Freel. The last sentence of this acknowledgment has long been reserved for T.A.C., my favorite trickster and cosmopolitan in the best sense of these terms, whose resourcefulness, patience, and love form the foundation of this book. Thank you for believing in me.

Tricksters and Cosmopolitans

Introduction

This book is about the production of the Asian cosmopolitan subject, dreamed into being by Asian American writers as it often is, through narrative fiction in the United States. The focus is not so much on the writers who are interested in celebrating this socially privileged figure, but on those who create a new critical standpoint from a transnational perspective *through* this figure. Placed front and center in the limelight, the cosmopolitan subject from Asia, equipped with transcendent transnational mobility and cultural capital, can easily obscure the more familiar but troubling figure of the Asian American working-class immigrant. Relegated to the margins of the narrative or banished to the realm of the past, irrelevance, and silence, the displaced working-class subject joins the ranks of other unprotected lives around the globe, whose lives are crushed by legacies of classic imperialisms in the earlier decades of the twentieth century and vulnerable to the exploitative forces of late capitalism. The Asian cosmopolitan subject is a convenient figure that can absolve the collective national consciousness of guilt involved in the shaping of conflicted histories that awaited its working-class Asian immigrants upon arrival in the United States. The figure can overwrite, for instance, the long struggles that the working-class immigrant communities endured to establish such fundamental human rights as citizenship. It can also distract attention from the history of discriminatory violence inflicted upon these communities, represented in extreme by incidents of mass detainment of the kind that took place on Angel Island and the internment camps nationwide during World War II. What most troubles me is that this is a figure that can provide us with relief from thinking about the ongoing realities of the laboring bodies of the Asian diaspora worldwide, the irreplaceable human costs revealed to us with an increasing number of reports about industrial accidents in outsourced factories that are run without the proper regulation that ensures the safety of its workers.

Literary analysis that examines the narrative construction of this cosmopolitan subject, by itself, would be inadequate in a book that claims to be about literary production. I also take into account the process involved in the material production of the literary works themselves, in the form of published texts. Taking a materialist approach to African American fiction in *Black Writers, White Publishers: Marketplace Politics in Twentieth- Century African American Literature* (2006), John K. Young emphasizes the restrictive role of editors and publishers in shaping the contours of African American writing, pointing to a dynamic in which "a concentration of money and cultural authority in mainstream publishers works to produce images of blackness that perpetuate an implicit black-white divide between authors and readers, with publishers acting as a gateway in this interaction."[1] I do not doubt that such demands of editors and publishers have been, and perhaps continue to be, a major compromising factor for minority writers; I even suspect that it would not be difficult to locate a similar dynamic in the process of publication for Asian American writers throughout the twentieth century. In my own materialist study, however, I choose to highlight cases in which the rapport between the Asian American writers and their non–Asian American editors and publishers can be reconceived as a process of creative collaboration. The (white) editors and publishers I discuss insisted—against the current—on the value of the works by Asian American writers, playing a crucial role as supporters and promoters who made it possible for new voices to emerge.

What the editors and publishers saw to be of value in the selection of primary texts varies in accordance with the outlets for the publication of each work, from literary fiction and literary magazines to printed mass media including mass-market popular fiction, outlets scattered across the dialectical spectrum of what Pierre Bourdieu called "autonomous" and "heteronomous" poles in the field of cultural production.[2] Their interests range from appreciation of avant-garde and other forms of literary achievement, sympathy with the political urgency of the social critique, to a recognition of the text's appeal to both the "sophisticated" and "average" reader on the level of affect and desire, holding up promises of commercial success. Some self-interest and ambition cannot be ruled out as incentives on the part of editors and publishers, but it also cannot be denied that all of the editors and publishers took on some degree of risk, financial and professional, in supporting the publication of the literary works in question. The earliest of these cross-cultural collaborations broke with the standard practices of the U.S. publishing industry, which traditionally rejected works by minority writers; the latest of the cross-cultural collaborations faced dramatic changes in the U.S. cultural landscape in the last few decades, reshaped by the dictates of neoliberal and global late capitalism.

The central notion of the writer as trickster in this book refers back to Henry Louis Gates Jr.'s *The Signifying Monkey: A Theory of African-American Literary Criticism* (1989), in which he introduces a mischievous trickster monkey from African American folktales as a unifying trope in theorizing the characteristic use of the black vernacular in African American literary tradition. As Gates explains, a string of African American trickster folk tales with the troublesome monkey is characterized by disruptive moments of "Signifying," which has very little to do with its meaning in Standard (white) English or with the Lacanian/Saussurean sense of the word but, rather, is a vernacular term that applies to a wide range of language games, figurative substitutions, and free associations that momentarily displaces the narrative itself to present "implicit formal critiques of language use." The term "Signifying" is itself a moment of "Signifying," since it contains a double entendre that is accessible only to those who are familiar with the black vernacular speech. The fact that the term retains the identical spelling of "its white counterpart" demonstrates that there is "a simultaneous, but negated, parallel discursive (ontological, political) universe [that] exists within the larger white discursive universe."[3]

If the African American vernacular can be seen as a language in its own right, as Gates does,[4] the literary critic Evelyn Nien-Ming Ch'ien might agree that the moments of "Signifying" in works by many African American writers including Zora Neale Hurston, Ishmael Reed, and Alice Walker constitute what she calls a "weirding" of English employed by a string of acclaimed immigrant and postcolonial writers of contemporary fiction such as Paul Beatty, Irvine Welsh, Derek Walcott, Paule Marshall, Junot Díaz, Li-Young Lee, Lois Ann Yamanaka, among others. Gates never claimed the trickster poetics of "Signifying" as an exclusive practice of black writers (95), nor was the idea of the trickster figure employed in rhetorical strategies and interpretation only relevant for black literary critics (53). "The implicit premise of this study is that all texts Signify upon other texts, in motivated and unmotivated ways," he wrote, before going on to suggest that "perhaps critics of other literatures will find this theory useful as they attempt to account for the configuration of the texts in their traditions" (xxiv–v).

In the writers' strategic use of the English vernacular inflected by each diaspora, what Ch'ien calls "weird English" momentarily displaces Standard (white) English, which "deprives English of its dominance and allows other languages to enjoy the same status":

> In literature, the conscious manipulation of English as subject matter is a balancing act of intelligibility and experiment. The best uses of weird English are terrible in their intelligibility, because they demonstrate that certain lives are linguistically disenfranchised and thus that some communities are excluded from mainstream discourse. To see, to read, to hear this awakens us to the voices that hide in the dark, waiting for ears to hear them.[5]

Wittgenstein's notion of language as *practice*, which undergirds Ch'ien's commentary here, is also central to Michel de Certeau's *The Practice of Everyday Life* (1984), a work that shifts the paradigm of discourse from producers of culture to the agency of users. De Certeau refers to the subversive practice of indigenous Indians who used imposed structure, including language, by the Spanish colonizers:

> Submissive, and even consenting to their subjection, the Indians nevertheless often *made of* the rituals, representations, and laws imposed on them something quite different from what their conquerors had in mind; they subverted them not by rejecting or altering them, but by using them with respect to ends and references foreign to the system they had no choice but to accept. They were the other within the very colonization that outwardly assimilated them; their use of the dominant social order deflected its power, which they lacked the means to challenge; they escaped it without leaving it.[6]

The indigenous Indians' strategic use and adaptation of a "system they had no choice but to accept," made to serve "their own interests and their own needs," is a practice of survival like "the immemorial intelligence displayed in the tricks and imitations of plants and fishes" (xix) and relevant also to the consumers of mass culture, "a marginal group which has now become a silent majority" (xvii), for whom "the unsigned, unreadable, and unsymbolized" activity of *use* is the only way to enact agency.

In de Certeau's formulation, "producers" and "users" are diametrically opposed categories, perhaps for the sake of clarity, so that ways of "reading" receive closer attention than ways of "writing." While the "weird English" writers are certainly producers of culture, one could argue that they are also "users" in a sense that they choose to write their works in English. On another level, they are also "users" who "Signify" upon the form of narrative fiction that emerges as an important mode of cultural expression in Western modernity. Gates identifies literature as the central arena in which persons of African descent "could, or could not, establish and redefine their status within the human community. Black people, the evidence suggests, had to represent themselves as 'speaking subjects' before they could even begin to destroy their status as objects, as commodities, within Western culture" (129). In parodic representation, writers "Signify" on an established literary form in such a way as to shift the reader's attention away from the semantic to the structural, rendering visible the particular rhetorical characteristic of a given literary form. African American writers might appropriate preexisting literary forms of Western modernity in order to create "a formal parody [that] suggests a given structure precisely by failing to coincide with it" (104). As Gates saw it, parodic representation simultaneously involves "a positioning or a critiquing both of received literary conventions and of the subject matter represented in canonical texts of the tradition" (113).[7] Two years earlier than Gates's *The Signifying Monkey*, for instance, Maxine Hong Kingston had created an iconoclastic protagonist in her novel *Tripmaster Monkey: His Fake Book* (1987) who embodies this notion of parodic repetition with a difference, in this vein aptly named Wittman Ah Sing. In Kingston's parodic representation, meaning is produced in part by revising formal patterns through this central character who, as Cyrus R. K. Patel recently wrote, seeks to revolutionize American literature by tapping into the transformative powers of the trickster figure from Wu-Cheng-en's sixteenth-century Chinese folk novel *Hsi Yu Chi* (*The Journey to the West*). Kingston's narrative can be read as a dramatization of typical struggles common to all U.S. late-twentieth-century minority cultures concerned with the "transform[ation of] themselves from marginal cultures into emergent cultures capable of challenging and reforming the mainstream."[8]

For Asian American writers, the art of silence has held a particular significance in playing an important role in their mode of "Signifying." In *The Signifying Monkey*, Gates's discussion of formal revision and implication in jazz and blues is of particular interest, especially when he explains that a downbeat can be created through its very absence.[9] In *Articulate Silences* (1993), King-Kok Cheung warned against the indiscriminate valorization of voice and speech prevalent in the stance of

Anglo-American feminist critics at the time, as well as the tendency of revisionist Asian male critics to reject silence altogether in their effort to refute the tired but still-existing stereotypes of the docile, submissive, and obedient "model minority." In the theoretical-philosophical realm, she argues, Augustine, Nietzsche, Heidegger, Picard, Wittgenstein, Foucault, Dauenhauer, and Derrida have all "in their own ways valorized speechlessness or displaced logocentricism"; in literature, there has always been an appreciation of irony, understatement, and other modes of implicit communication apparent in the writings of Susan Sontag, Stephen R. Portch, Janis P. Stout, and J. A. Ward. Silence can itself speak, and "Signify": "The art of silencecovers various 'strategies of reticence' (Janice Stout's term)—irony, hedging, coded language, muted plots—used by women writers to tell the forbidden and name the unspeakable."[10] Effective use of silence can serve as a means for defamiliarization, which, as Bertolt Brecht saw it, provided an alternative realism to the realist novel he rejected, with its harmonious fully rounded characters ("the individual") and linear narrative ("progress"), as an essentially bourgeois concept rooted in Western modernity.[11]

In the first chapter, I show how "Signifying" operates in literary works by writers who are almost always considered to be "the first" writers of African American literature and Asian American literature respectively: Charles Chesnutt and Sui Sin Far. While *Tricksters and Cosmopolitans* is conceived as a scholarly work on Asian American literary production, I take some liberty in taking the space that is necessary to demonstrate first that the emergence of African American literature, shaped by the specific historical-material condition in Jim Crow America at the turn of the last century, is a useful template for understanding the cultural dynamic that brought Asian American literary production into being at an also turbulent time of overwhelming anti-Chinese sentiment throughout the nation. In both the stories included in Chesnutt's *Conjure Woman* (1899) and Sui Sin Far's short stories also published at the turn of the last century, the writers perform "double-voiced" acts of signification, both within the narrative structure itself and in the presentation of the authors' identity. While defining "trickster" discourse necessitated by the cultural borders that have to be crossed or transgressed covertly for communication to succeed, this chapter underscores the indispensable presence of Chesnutt's editor, Walter Hines Page, and Sui Sin Far's editor at the *Independent*, William Hayes Ward, who each played a key role in the enabling and shaping of the writers' literary careers.

The second chapter turns to San Francisco during the early 1970s, situating the Filipino American writer Jessica Hagedorn in relationship to pioneering literary movements in the Bay Area, including avant-garde poetry, the Black Arts movement, the emerging Chicano/Latino literary movement, to Second Wave/Third World feminist literature. Existing scholarly accounts of these movements have accomplished much in delineating each movement in detail and showing them to be distinctive in its politics and aesthetics. Yet versatile writers like Hagedorn were actually able to move in and out of multiple literary scenes, participating in events where key writers from seemingly separate movements came into direct contact with one another to form extraordinary moments of collective creative energy.[12] While the poet Kenneth Rexroth is almost always invoked as Hagedorn's mentor, recently acquired archival material from UC Berkeley's Bancroft Library (Jessica Hagedorn Papers and Momo's Press Papers) attests to the presence of other mediating figures who promoted Hagedorn's writing at the beginning of her literary career. Chief among them was a San Francisco native poet named Stephen Vincent, who was a pioneering figure in working with artists across established boundaries of race and ethnicity, both as the California state coordinator for the Poetry in the Schools Program (1971–73) and as the editor and publisher of the small literary publishing house Momo's Press (1972–81).[13] It was Vincent who published the first two volumes of Hagedorn's poems, and as I discuss later, he also made significant contributions in the shaping of her 1981 novella "Pet Food."

In this chapter, I discuss the narrative construction of the cosmopolitan subject through the literary analysis of the novella and sketch out the concerns it registers about the emerging structure of globalization. In the novella, the seemingly standard bildungsroman narrative of the Filipino American protagonist named George Sand is written in a way that allows us to perceive a problematic convention of the novelistic form: the dynamic of center-periphery and the privileging of a linear narrative of "progress" contingent on the rejection of tradition and the past. In Hagedorn's novella, the making of the Filipino artist as the privileged modern subject happens alongside the death of a working-class Filipino American musician character who is killed off as an embodiment of *difference* and "the past." The realist novel has indeed been a useful medium for the modern subject to be conceived as speaking subjects; it has offered an effective way of "writing" previously ignored voices into "being," challenging the dehumanizing historical conditions created by Western modernity. Yet that new subjectivity brought into being itself brings a new set of marginalizations, disavowals, and projections of its own, so that these articulations might become, however unwittingly, an act of betrayal to those for whom this new speaking subject pretends to advocate.

One important issue raised through "Pet Food" is the implication of the culture industry at large with the workings of late capitalism, rendering any writer who engages successfully in cultural production vulnerable to the criticism that the act of writing reinforces a socioeconomic status quo that is problematic, regardless of well-meaning politics. For instance, in describing the typical attack on Henry Louis Gates Jr. himself "as a scholar whose ascendance was indeed made possible by his stated intention to rewrite black vernacular speech as literary theory," Kenneth W. Warren makes a stunning point:

> Gates made it clear in *The Signifying Monkey: A Theory of Afro-American Literature* (1988) that a set of rather bleak social-economic indicators—the replacement of de jure by de facto segregation of "black and white schoolchildren" coupled with a rate of "black unemployment in 1988 . . . much higher than it was in 1968"—provided the context for his claims that the black vernacular was "thriving despite predictions during the civil rights era that it would soon be a necessary casualty of school desegregation and the larger socioeconomic integration of black people into mainstream American institutions" (xix). The viability of the black vernacular is *literally underwritten* by the very conditions that Gates laments as having created two black Americas, separate and unequal.[14] (emphasis mine)

This commentary resonates with the self-addressed criticism that some Asian American writers face individually as Third World writers. The novelistic structure, in which the fullness and centrality of a modern subjectivity occurs through silencing, marginalization, and *othering* of the many, in fact serves as a direct metaphor for the way in which the privileged global citizens of "Empire," in Michael Hardt and Antonio Negri's sense,[15] claim entitlement to centrality by exploiting (silencing, marginalizing, and *othering*) both the underprivileged local population and those in the outlying colonies of formerly imperialist nation-states. As Trinh T. Minh-ha reminds us in *Woman, Native, Other* (1989), the Third World female writer must live with a constant reminder of those who never come to writing; for the act of writing is itself "always practiced at the cost of other women's labor."[16] In her materialist consideration of postcolonial literary production in the United Kingdom, Sarah Brouillette points out in *Postcolonial Writers in the Global Literary Marketplace* (2007) that the postcolonial author emerges in the global literary market, in orientation and in location catering to Anglo-American readers with access to "privileged metropolitan markets," as "a profoundly complicit and compromised figure whose authority rests, however uncomfortably, in the nature of his connection to the specificity of a given political location."[17]

This second chapter, on Jessica Hagedorn's work, is meant to lead up to further engagement with literary production under global capitalism in the third chapter. In contemporary texts by three Asian American writers, Karen Tei Yamashita, Monique Truong, and Min Jin Lee, the cosmopolitan figure in narrative fiction registers the writers' acute concern over the oppressiveness of the historical condition shaped by globalization. As Rachel Lee asserted at the cusp of the new century, "one of the most—if not the most—pressing social concerns informing Asian American cultural critique in the 1990s is globalization and the prospects of an Asian-Pacific community amid increasing transnational traffic."[18] In Yamashita's experimental novel *Tropic of Orange* (1998), the inanimate object of the orange and other commodities in global circulation ("gifts of NAFTA") become a shorthand for the silencing and marginalization inherent in the traditional structure of the novel, also imbued with the historical displacement of the large number of working-class laborers in transnational circulation. In the case of Monique Truong's *The Book of Salt* (2004), a novel staged in Gertrude Stein's salon in Paris, the silent "Indochinese" cooks in Alice B. Toklas's cookbook are temporarily granted speech and centrality in the form of Stein's Vietnamese cook, Bình. Extremely powerful historical figures from South Asia make their appearances as Asian cosmopolitan subjects in the novel: the emperor of Vietnam, Crown Prince Norodom (Sihanouk) of Cambodia, and the unnamed "scholar-prince" whom David Eng aptly reads as "one Nguyen That Thanh also known as Nguyen Ai Quoc," or, Ho Chi Minh.[19] That these individuals are in turn reduced to fleeting figures in Truong's novel is an important part of her larger criticism to be gleaned from her novel about how the current U.S.-led globalization builds itself on the legacies of earlier imperialisms in the twentieth century.

The critique of globalization in Min Jin Lee's *Free Food for Millionaires* (2007) takes an altogether different track, using the Asian cosmopolitan subject to show the exploitation of the middle class in the United States unleashed by the deregulation of the financial sector starting in the 1980s. The resubjugation of formerly colonized parts of the world though outsourcing of labor by transnational corporations headquartered in global cities (many in the United States) is not the only mode of profit extraction in neoliberal capitalism; the subsequent job loss of workers in the manufacturing sector and increasingly in the white-collar industry within the United States, while equally heartrending, is not the only casualty. As Saskia Sassen explains, profits are also extorted from "unlikely domains including subprime mortgages on modest residences or through unlikely instruments, such as credit default swaps, a key component of the shadow banking system,"[20] which ultimately led to the financial crisis of 2008. In Lee's novel, cultural capital (BA in economics from Princeton) does not actually guarantee much financial stability for the Korean American protagonist, Casey Han, once she leaves the home of her immigrant family. She is driven deeper and deeper into credit-card debt, trying to prove her global citizenship status through conspicuous consumption, which she thinks will protect her from various forms of *othering*. That Casey takes out even more loans to cover her business school tuition at NYU in order to gain a "better" position at one of the largest firms in Wall Street is painfully ironic, since she puts herself in a position to be exploited as a worker as well as the consumer, unknowingly perpetuating the very system that funds and keeps her indentured to the stronghold of the credit-card industry.

This final chapter does not offer detailed editorial exchanges that took place during the publication of these books, mostly for lack of access to such material. However, the chapter delineates the new political contours of cross-cultural collaboration set against the drastic changes in the publishing industry under global capitalism. From the 1960s onward, major publishing houses experienced fast-paced corporate mergers that ultimately placed all of them under the control of multinational conglomerates. While these mergers offered a viable solution for the publishing houses to compete among themselves, the presses found that they were expected to generate double-digit shareholder profit equal to other branches of the culture industry.[21] Under the ruthless logic of financialized global capitalism under neoliberalism starting in the 1980s, as the cultural anthropologist Karen Ho explains in *Liquidated: An Ethnography of Wall Street* (2009), the identity of a corporation no longer rests on the employees themselves but on its shareholders often *at the cost of* the employees. Many editors and publishers who worked in the U.S. mainstream publishing industry became precariously positioned within a fluctuating terrain now driven by the demands of the financial sector's singular focus on shareholder profits. Against this background, André Schiffrin convincingly and movingly argued in *The Business of Books: How the International Conglomerates Took over Publishing and Changed the Way We Read* (1999) that global capitalism threatens the pursuit of truth and the defense of foundational democratic principles traditionally at the core of the publishing business.

Under these circumstances, one might find a newly added impetus for cross-cultural collaboration in publishing works that offer sophisticated critiques of globalization. This chapter maps out the distinctive positions of editor-publishers working for a nonprofit independent publishing house, a major literary publishing house, and a major commercial publishing house. Coffee House Press, which published *Tropic of Orange*, was run by a former poet and letterpress owner, the late Allan Kornblum, who had actively embraced literary innovation and was open to politically charged works, and it is possible to see a strong political resonance between Karen Tei Yamashita's critique of globalization and Kornblum's own outspokenness about the debilitating competition against major presses housed under conglomerates, often with access to their own distribution networks and possessing enough capital to cut deals with chain bookstores. In the case of Monique Truong's *The Book of Salt*, a high level of literary sophistication would have been important to her editor, Janet Silver, at the time the vice president of the major literary publishing house Houghton Mifflin. Having published Jhumpa Lahiri's highly acclaimed and best-selling short-story collection *The Interpreter of Maladies* (1999), Silver had established a solid reputation for captivating the niche global market of postcolonial literature. Similarly, some level of literary sophistication would also have been important to Min Jin Lee's editor, Amy Einhorn, who started out her career at a literary publishing house (Farrar, Straus and Giroux). But at the time of publishing Lee's *Free Food for Millionaires*, Einhorn was working for Warner Books (later renamed Grand Central Publishing), which had historically developed as a commercial publishing house. Einhorn was working to cultivate a new imprint there (5 Spot) geared toward the hugely lucrative chick-lit industry intended for a mass female audience.[22]

The spectacular commercial success of Silver and Einhorn as editors at the turn of the new century, in the global postcolonial literary and the mass popular fiction marketplace, should not immediately cancel out the possibility of a shared critical stance toward globalization. The global postcolonial literary marketplace is made up of an audience that Brouillette describes as a set of "cosmopolitan, elite readers of English-language literary fiction . . . who are *literary* in a way that Timothy Brennan identifies as the 'complexities and subtleties' of a very specific kind of 'great art'" (58, 59).[23] At its worst, this audience can be defined by some negative characteristics associated with cosmopolitanism, such as exclusivity, privileged dilettantism, and apolitical irresponsibility. These same negative characteristics of the cosmopolitan audience can be found in a different form if we consider the audience for mass-market chick-lit fiction who delight in the stories featuring extravagant shopping excursions, the pleasure of which comes from the confirmation of their own "discerning" taste in high-end designer offerings without having to think about the realities of low-wage manufacturing workers who actually produce those commodities under extortionist conditions in postcolonial spaces. In both these cases, the trickster writer might be appropriating the very principles of free-market cosmopolitanism that reorganize the division of labor on a global scale under multinational corporate capitalism while actually cultivating countervailing alliances and networks through literary production.

Tricksters and Cosmopolitans does not offer a comprehensive account of Asian American publishing history, but it does aim to address the most glaring absence in current scholarship on the publishing history of Asian American writing. Laura Hyun Yi Kang's *Compositional Subjects: Enfiguring Asian/American Women* (2002), for instance, offers an excellent overview of Asian American publishing history in terms of Asian American women writers during the 1970s and 1980s contributing to the identification of "Asian women," "Asian American women," and "Asian Pacific American women," used as terms that coalesced through social, political, and cultural formations through Asian American periodicals like *Gidra*, *Amerasia Journal*, and *Bridge: An Asian American Perspective*, or anthologies from UC Berkeley's *Asian Women* (1971) to *Making Waves: An Anthology of Writings by and about Asian American Women* (1989), which responded to the frustrations about their lack of voice and visibility. By contrast, the existing scholarship on Asian American writing in "mainstream" (white) publishing industry is very slim, consisting of Tetsuden Kashima and Naomi B. Pascal's "In Press: Publishing on the Asian American Experience" in the *Journal of Reading* (1987) and Mindy Okura and Jill Su's "The Asian American Market for Publishers in the United States" in *Publishing Research Quarterly* (2003). While these articles provide insightful explanations for the growing number of publications in Asian American literature, they are limited in identifying the marketing opportunities that they see as determining factor for these publications, be it a response to the rapid development of ethnic studies curricula from the late 1960s (Kashima and Pascal) or the discovery of Asian American fiction's marketability in the 1990s proven by the massive success of such novels as Amy Tan's *Joy Luck Club* in 1987 (Okura and Su).

What is currently lacking is a discussion beyond ethnic or racial identity politics in the publishing history of Asian American literary works. In Kang's analysis of Maxine Hong Kingston's *The Woman Warrior*, for instance, the Knopf editor's infamous designation of the novel as "autobiography" opens up a rich discussion about the tension between the commodification of authenticity and Kingston's "writing self." From a business perspective, the Knopf editor is not entirely wrong in making that call, as the successful publications of Asian American writing earlier in the twentieth century had indeed been autobiographies: Etsu Sugimoto's *A Daughter of the Samurai* (1925) and *A Daughter of Narikin* (1932), Miné Okubo's *Citizen 13660* (1944), Carlos Bulosan's *America Is in the Heart* (1946), Jade Snow Wong's *Fifth Chinese Daughter* (1950), and Monica Sone's *Nisei Daughter* (1953), among others. However, Kingston's *The Woman Warrior* was not actually featured as autobiography when was first published. What later became the first chapter of *The Woman Warrior* appeared first as a short story entitled "No Name Woman" in *Viva: The International Magazine for Women*, initially published in 1973 as one of the first women's magazines that featured female erotica along with articles and fiction focused on women's fantasies.[24] There, the power of Kingston's writing lends itself to what was an attempt to destabilize existing boundaries of gender and was an active part of a cross-cultural collaboration to bring change to the U.S. cultural landscape. This historical dimension of Kingston's writing resists the paradigmatic discussion of her text within the confines of identity politics based on race and ethnicity, which her writing was actually able to transcend.

In engaging with the relationship between aesthetics, social critique, and historical condition through the discussion of various cross-cultural collaborations, my work builds on the rapidly growing interest in studying the aesthetics and literary form in Asian American writing that can be seen in essay collections such as *Literary Gestures: The Aesthetic in Asian American Literature,* edited by Rocio G. Davis and Sue-Im Lee (2003), and *Form and Transformation: In Asian American Literature*, edited by Xiaojing Zhou and Samina Najmi (2005). Scholars working with Asian American poetry, such as Josephine Park, Yunte Huang, and Timothy Yu, have produced important scholarly works that focus on Asian American writers' engagement with aesthetics. Yu's *Race and the Avant-Garde* (2009), for instance, provocatively makes a case that issues of aesthetic experimentation and innovation were as central a concern for Asian American poets as for their contemporary avant-garde poets. While these works offer excellent explorations of Asian American poetry, issues of aesthetics can surely be just as important to Asian American writers of narrative fiction. At the very least, they deserve equal attention in literary studies.

The plural form in the title *Tricksters and Cosmopolitans* reflects the fluidity and multiplicity in the designations in my use of these terms, applied inside and outside of the literary text. While the book is about the construction of the Asian cosmopolitan subject, the writers are themselves cosmopolitan subjects with the ability to manipulate two diverse, and at times antagonistic, cultural codes; the enabling (white) editors and publishers of these writers are also cosmopolitan, as advocates of cross-cultural communication straddling the familiar and the unfamiliar, the known and the unknown, the visible and the invisible (whether or not they fully appreciate the creative slippage of language which is always present). Most tellingly in the case of the cross-cultural literary production from a major commercial publishing house, a radical political alignment between the Asian American writer and non–Asian American editor and publisher with regard to globalization may be too much to hope for. But even then, at least in the publication of Min Jin Lee's novel by Amy Einhorn, some element of creative collaboration can be found on the part of the editor-publisher who is invested in diversifying a genre of mass women's fiction with a protagonist who is not the default white middle-class single woman.

My choice to focus on *cosmopolitans* rather than *cosmopolitanism* indicates a certain distance between this book and the critical discourse surrounding cosmopolitanism claimed by multiple scholarly fields including philosophy, the social sciences, political theory, and legal scholarship, with an emphasis on issues of global governance, citizenship, and human rights. I have nothing but admiration for the important work established by scholars including Kwame Anthony Appiah, Martha Nussbaum, David Held, Michael Waltzer, Bruce Robbins, among others. Still, I would have to agree with Susan Koshy that it seems impossible for most scholarly discussion of cosmopolitanism to disarticulate itself from its heavily European genealogy and the tendency to remain Eurocentric.[25] This is true even of Pheng Cheah's intervention in *Inhuman Conditions: On Cosmopolitanism and Human Rights* (2006), which carefully considers the limitations of classic cosmopolitanisms as seen in the writing of Immanuel Kant and Jürgen Habermas.

Cheah's criticisms about the shortfalls of the more "radical" cosmopolitanisms of James Clifford and Homi Bhabha are inspiring, however, grounded as they are squarely within the historical conditions of globalization. When Cheah briefly touches upon literature (among other arts), it is as a medium that promotes cosmopolitanism through "the constructive, artificial (*künstlich*) powers of the imagination," which works against parochialism by broadening the readers' perspectives and widening the circle of belonging through the process of identification. Of the several sophisticated criticisms on the process of identification, as laid out by Diana Fuss in *Identification Papers* (1995), an important point to keep in mind is Judith Butler's remark that identification is often "purchased through a set of constitutive and formative exclusions."[26] Most often it would be "exclusions" of the subaltern subjects in decolonized space, whom I believe Cheah cares about the most, "who have no access to globality and who view coerced economic migration as a plus" and situated "outside the circuit of the international division of labor and must bear the impact of global-systemic inequality on food production, consumption, and superexploitation outside wage labor."[27] Rita Felski's argument in *Uses of Literature* (2008) reframes identification within a broader phenomenology of recognition, in which one might "confirm and intensify a sense of particularity, but it may also cut across and confuse familiar rubrics of identity." As she writes, "recognition is about knowing, but also about the limits of knowing and knowability, and about how self-perception is mediated by the other, and the perception of otherness by the self."[28] Within the process of recognition, then, world literature might provide a reader with the kind of promising encounter described by Appiah, a cultivation of cosmopolitan sensibility through defamiliarizing reading experiences rather than through identification, when "values of others that we had not previously recognized or that can undermine our commitment to values that we had settled into."[29]

During the years leading up to my completion of *Tricksters and Cosmopolitans*, an alarming new development in globalization started to take shape in the form of two proposed new free trade agreements negotiated behind closed doors by both U.S. political parties and the corporate elites, with their counterparts in other countries in the Pacific Rim and the EU: The Trans-Pacific Participation (TPP) and Trans-Atlantic Free Trade Agreement (TAFTA). Overcoming a major opposition from his key constituents including trade unions, environmentalists, and Latino organizations, President Barack Obama secured Fast Track trade negotiation authority in 2015.[30] As leading economists like Jeffrey Sachs and trade activist Lori Wallach have argued, these are not trade treaties but agreements aimed at protecting investors, with far-reaching consequences on existing regulations covering environmental protection, food safety, Internet freedom, and labor conditions, as well as public access to essential services like water, electricity, and gas, all the while promoting privatization of public works and financial deregulation. In the words of Nobel laureate Joseph Stiglitz, "corporations may profit [from the TPP], and it is even possible, though far from assured, that gross domestic product as conventionally measured will increase. But the well-being of ordinary citizens is likely to take a hit."[31]

By far the most urgent concern is the invester-state dispute settlement (ISDS) clause built into the FTA, allowing investors (i.e., corporations) to challenge the very sovereignty of a given nation-state. According to the leaked documents, under the proposed ISDS clause, if a particular legislation of a participating nation can be argued as being harmful to profit projected by a given corporation, the investors are permitted to sue that government in an international tribunal. So it is that the pharmaceutical giant Eli Lilly filed a $500 million lawsuit under the North American Free Trade Agreement (NAFTA) against the Canadian government on September 13, 2013, for allowing Canadian courts to invalidate patents for two of its drugs. This lawsuit was filed in addition to Eli Lilly's earlier NAFTA lawsuit against Canada over its cautious regulations for clinical study necessary to permit its drugs to be on the market, claiming that this has cost them more than $1 billion, curbing its revenue in 2012 to a "mere" $4 billion.[32] If the Canadian government loses this NAFTA lawsuit, it will be required to amend its laws to prevent similar lawsuits in the future. This calls into question the very sovereignty of the nation-state, since foreign investors' interests can overrule domestic court decisions. In the face of such a dark future choreographed by forces of global capitalism, it seems ever more important to recall the cross-cultural collaborations in literary production that are at times also enabled by globalization, to light up the paths that lead to forgotten, buried, or hidden moments of human agency, daring and brilliant.

1 / Trickster Poetics at the Turn of the Twentieth Century

In order to understand the cultural dynamic that has shaped Asian American literary production during the last decades of the twentieth century and the beginning of the twenty-first, it may be useful to consider its emergence at the previous turn of century, and to consider a template. This chapter begins with a discussion of the trickster figure that surfaces as African American literature emerged, building on Henry Louis Gates Jr.'s *The Signifying Monkey*, the first work to theorize the rhetorical strategy of tricksters as a unifying trope in African American literature. The first African American novelist to capture the attention of the literary world was, by general consensus, Charles Chesnutt. *The Conjure Woman* (1899), his first and most commercially successful literary work, is narrated through a double-voice that casts him in the role of a "trickster" author. The relationship between Chesnutt and his editors at the *Atlantic*, that of Walter Hines Page in particular, allows us access to a particular form of cosmopolitanism in New England that contributed to a major shift in the national imaginary. While the *Atlantic* has rightly been criticized for its (white male) exclusivity and elitism, the interracial collaboration over literary production surrounding Chesnutt's work broke new ground in the magazine's antislavery stance, enacting egalitarian and democratic ideals at a time of increasing racial violence in Jim Crow America.

If African American literature emerged from the fraught historical condition of Jim Crow America, a different line was being drawn definitively between white America and the Chinese in the United States around that time. The Chinese Exclusion Act of 1882, barring entry of all Chinese immigrants, had been renewed with stricter provisions with the Geary Act in 1892. When it came up for another renewal in 1902, Congress voted this time to make it permanent. The Chinese Exclusion Act crystallized the extreme hostility toward the Chinese in the United States, which had otherwise taken the form of mob violence that swept through the West Coast during the last decades of the nineteenth century.[1] While Jim Crow laws and anti-Chinese exclusion laws were very different in many ways, they share a strangely similar structure of feeling expressed in spatial terms. Historically, they both occur at a heightened moment when U.S. imperialism starts to take shape, with the pivotal shift at the end of Spanish-American War in 1898 when new territories were no longer absorbed as a part of the nation but remained foreign: Puerto Rico, the Philippines, and Guam. Amy Kaplan suggests in *Anarchy of Empire in the Making of U.S. Culture* (2005) that the ambiguity and contradiction of these newly acquired territories, which are a part of the United States as an empire but not a part of the United States as a nation, played itself out in the formation of national culture. The indeterminacy caused by the dual borders now imagined between the United States and the rest of the world might explain the extreme need to police the preexisting lines of race and citizenship. This chapter turns to the short stories of Sui Sin Far, the first writer of Chinese descent to address a national audience in the United States at the turn of the century, focusing particularly on her publications between 1909 and 1913 in the *Independent*. A journal that came out of the abolition movement in New England, the *Independent* under William Hayes Ward's editorship exhibited nonorientalist interest and open-mindedness to the Chinese in the United States that was exceedingly rare at that time in U.S. history.

In his classic study on the canonicity of African American literature that centers around slave narratives, *(Dis)forming the American Canon: African-Arabic Slave Narratives and the Vernacular* (1993), Ronald A. T. Judy justly issues a caveat about the way in which the notion of "writing the self into being" reveals Western modernity's problematic but dominant typology of signs, or the "economy of signification in which there is necessary relationship between literacy and reflective consciousness": The very logic that requires a (black) man to "validate his humanity through literacy, that makes writing the sole avenue to humanity" is indeed disturbing when the African subjectivity brought into being through the writing self represents "an emancipating death . . . the negation of the materiality of Africa";[2] Olaudah Equiano, who wrote *The Interesting Narrative of the Life of Olaudah Equiano or Gustavus Vassa, the African, Written by Himself* (1789), might gain voice and emerge from "the abject muteness of objectivity into productive subjectivity" but with a cost, as "the muted African body is overwritten by the Negro, and the Negro that emerges in the ink flow of Equiano's pen is that which has overwritten itself and so become the representation of the very body it sits on" (89).[3]

This dynamic in which a sacrifice of the racialized and muted body becomes necessary in producing the speaking subject is indeed an important one. In chapter 2, I pursue this notion of *thanatology* in discussing how such sacrificial disavowals are projected outward in Jessica Hagedorn's "Pet Food." For the moment, Judy's commentary serves to show the adversarial historical conditions that an African American or an Asian writer like Chesnutt and Sui Sin Far were up against, necessitating the creation of "Signifying" narratives that seemingly subscribe to the ideology imposed by Western modernity while covertly subverting it. I would also point out that Equiano's literacy and the ink flow of his pen are not enough to make him a "speaking subject." In chapter 3, I try to stop perpetuating the invisibility of those who contribute to making these critically charged narratives available for the general readership. Produced somewhat earlier than the time period Pierre Bourdieu has in mind in *The Field of Cultural Production*, Equiano's narrative was made possible by 308 subscribers who put money up front for its publication. This group included the Prince of Wales and the Duke of York, so perhaps these are people whose very social privilege and relative visibility make up for the lack of acknowledgment. But even in the case of editor-publishers Walter Hines Page and William Hayes Ward, who respectively played a large role in introducing the writing of Charles Chesnutt and Sui Sin Far, I argue that we are looking at mediators whose contributions in shaping the cultural terrain in the United States deserve due appreciation, free of cynicism or reactionary accusation, in bringing the "speaking subject" into being.

Locating Trickster Poetics: Charles Chesnutt's *The Conjure Woman* (1899) and Walter Hines Page

A curious disavowal of political resonance in the term "Jim Crow" occurs in Charles W. Chesnutt's "Goophered Grapevine," a short story published in the *Atlantic* in 1887. In this "conjure story" set in the antebellum South, a powerful spell ("goopher") is cast upon an old slave named Henry, whose physical health begins to reflect the seasonal vicissitudes of the grapevines of a former plantation. Just as young leaves begin to sprout in the spring, hair starts growing on Henry's bald head, curling up into tight little balls; by the time the grapes are fully ripe, his head looks "des like a bunch er grapes."[4] Uncle Julius, the ex-slave who tells this story in regional dialect, describes Henry struggling to take control of his hair, working half the night "wid er Jim Crow" (with a Jim Crow) only to find that it had grown back into the tight, grape-like curls. From the first 1899 edition of *The Conjure Woman*, a notation of the term "Jim Crow" appears in a footnote right at the bottom of the page, promptly informing the reader that "Jim Crow" is "A small card, resembling a currycomb in construction, and used by negroes in the rural districts instead of a comb." The term "Jim Crow" is thus to be taken in its most literal meaning, referring to a type of comb, his reader is led to believe, absolved of all concerns about the Jim Crow laws of racial segregation in post-Reconstruction South, or the related bombings, lynchings, and mob violence characteristic of the backlash against the gains of African Americans in the Reconstruction era. At most, the readers may have thought of the "Jump Jim Crow" character in minstrel shows reaching back to Thomas Dartmouth Rice's blackface minstrelsy in 1828. This would have suggested that a racist undertone might be found at play in the volume, directing attention away from the actual political nature of Chesnutt's writing. Only a handful of his readers in the North may have known enough to consider the crucial role of the comb as a means of establishing one's racial identity for county records,[5] or as something used in a grooming procedure for slaves that was at times accompanied by physical pain.[6]

Scholars have commented on the double structure in Chesnutt's narratives that hides a potentially incendiary political commentary for readers looking to find it. This double structure tells us much about the constraints of the first pioneering African American writer in the late nineteenth century, constraints that shape another double structure over the racial identity Chesnutt presented to his audience. The northern acquiescence to southern control of the "Negro problem" and its effective condoning of blatant acts of white-supremacist assault occurring in the South, as Eric Sundquist has written, ensnared African American artists in a "constant awareness and estimation of the effect of the color line upon his professional aspirations and his literary materials," a dilemma highlighted for writers like Chesnutt who "emblematically incorporated the essence of the race crisis" that "dictated the perspective of much of his fiction."[7] Although Chesnutt himself never concealed his African American ancestry from his editors, it was not always made clear to the readers of his books. Writing in the 1950s, Sterling A. Brown asserted that Chesnutt's racial identity was seen to have been "concealed by his publishers who feared that knowledge that he was a Negro would injure his reception in a market where there was a high premium on books *about* Negroes but not by Negroes."[8] The *Atlantic Monthly* did in fact run William Deans Howells's review essay that mentions Chesnutt's "sixteenth part of a race,"[9] and also acknowledged Chesnutt's African American ancestry in introducing his short story. Even there, Chesnutt is referred to as "a coloured man of very light complexion" following a hyperbolic appeal to the audience that "*the most tragic situation in fiction that has ever been conceived in this country* is that in which a mulatto finds himself with all the qualities of the white race in a position where he must suffer from the disadvantages of the coloured race" (emphasis mine).[10] In his 1889 letter to the writer Albion Tourgée, the attorney who made the case against Jim Crow laws in *Plessy v. Ferguson*, Chesnutt expresses hopefulness that "the fact of color" would not hurt his literary career: "If I have the patience and the industry to pursue [the road to success in literature], the fact of color may in the course of time prove to be a distinction instead of a disadvantage."[11] However, Chesnutt also highlights his whiteness in writing of himself that "the infusion of African blood is very small—is not in fact a visible admixture," in his letter to Houghton Mifflin two years later.[12] This is very different from W. E. B. DuBois's identification of his racial identity in the haunting last sentence to "Forethought" in *The Souls of Black Folk* (1903): "need I add that I who speak here am bone of the bone and flesh of the flesh of them that live within the Veil?"

Set in post-Reconstruction North Carolina, Chesnutt's collection of short stories in *The Conjure Woman* has the appearance of conforming to a set of established conventions found in the nineteenth-century plantation tales popularized by writers like Joel Chandler Harris, Thomas Nelson Page, and Harry Stillwell. Presenting romanticized and nostalgic sketches of a rustic South in which simple-minded and uncomplaining slaves are slotted into paternalistic white society, plantation tales usually featured antebellum stories told in "authentic" local dialect by a black character, contained within the "frame story" of a white narrator who speaks in Standard English. In *The Conjure Woman*, a character named Uncle Julius tells fanciful "conjure" tales from slavery time that he had "be'n hearin' . . . fer twenty-five yeahs," since his childhood, when he "wa'n't mo'd'n knee-high ter a hopper-grass" (101). Each story is introduced by a white narrator, John, a northerner who moves his wine business from northern Ohio to the war-ravaged South. John's frame story provides a seemingly "rational" counterpoint to the fantastical stories told by Uncle Julius, usually ending with some form of commentary that suggests that Uncle Julius's stories always hide some shrewd ulterior motive of his own. In plantation fiction, the white narrator is thus given the ability to determine the context while the black character remains silenced, and this has been seen as an implicit endorsement of racist ideology. As Robert C. Nowatzki notes, John's frame story serves the function of containing "any challenge that Julius poses to dominant ideologies of slavery and racial difference," reaffirming readers' beliefs in white authority, racial difference, and black inferiority.[13] Accordingly, stories like "The Goophered Grapevine" and "The Gray Wolf's Han't" assure readers that John's entrepreneurial ambitions, in buying or developing the former plantation, are never thwarted by Uncle Julius's tales.

Needless to say, the fin de siècle was a deeply disturbing time at the peak of lynchings,[14] along with the reinstatement of interracial marriage bans in all seven states in the Lower South,[15] and the increasing codification of segregated public spaces leading up to the 1896 landmark Supreme Court decision in *Plessy v. Ferguson*, which legally sanctioned laws in the Jim Crow South designating schools, public transportation, hotels, and other public buildings as "white" or "colored." In North Carolina, where Chesnutt ran his stenography firm and aspired to a practice as a lawyer while writing his short stories and novels, a particularly violent riot occurred in Wilmington on November 10, 1898, destroying many black-owned businesses and running many black families out of their homes.[16] In a letter to his publishing editor at Houghton Mifflin, Walter Hines Page, Chesnutt refers to the Wilmington riots as an "outbreak of pure, malignant and altogether indefensible race prejudice which makes me feel personally humiliated, and ashamed for the country and the State."[17] In *The Marrow of Tradition* (1901), Chesnutt would go on to openly challenge the logic of segregation that promoted lynchings as well as the riots.[18] *The Marrow of Tradition* could not have been published without the considerable success of *The Conjure Woman*, a work that had gained a kind of phenomenal popularity that his second book did not, by keeping the harshest point of his social critique largely obscured. Chesnutt's ability to launch a social critique of any sort depended first on his position as a popular writer at the turn of the century, a position secured by "his ability to fulfill his readers' desires, and his willingness to challenge their expectations only subtly."[19]

That Chesnutt's stories contain an implicit critique of this structure is perhaps most apparent in the way that John's frame story creates discernible distortions. John's skepticism leads readers away from the actual fact that Uncle Julius's allegedly cunning pursuit of self-interest involves helping members of his family and friends, rather than being motivated by selfishness. Through his storytelling, Uncle Julius secures an old schoolhouse on the property as space for his newly seceded congregation ("Po' Sandy") and successfully rallies to keep his grandson employed in John's household ("Mars Jeems's Nightmare"). In some stories, Uncle Julius's only motive seems to be the sympathy he feels for John's family members, as in an instance in which his storytelling helps John's wife, Annie, overcome her depression ("Sis' Becky's Pickaninny") or when his storytelling serves to patch up a troublesome quarrel between Annie's sister and her fiancé ("Hot-Foot Hannibal"). In one particular story that significantly shapes readers' perception of Uncle Julius, "The Conjuror's Revenge," John's narrative implies that Uncle Julius must have taken part in a scheme to swindle John of money, in brokering the purchase of a horse from his friend. Immediately after the sale, the horse's health deteriorates so rapidly that John says "a more worthless, broken-winded, spavined quadruped never disgraced the noble name of horse" (130); it dies "in a fit of colic" after two or three months. Somewhat resentfully, John casts suspicion that Uncle Julius deceived him so he could buy himself a new suit of the latest style, a suit that John himself had also been eyeing. But even if Uncle Julius *had* received money from his friend after the sale of the horse, there is ample room to think that what had transpired was an honest brokering on Uncle Julius's part to help his friend with the sale of a horse. It seems just as plausible for Uncle Julius not to have been able to foresee that the horse would lose its health, given that John himself thought of the horse as "a very fine-looking animal" at the time of the sale. Yet John's narrative is told in a way that makes such reasoning appear hopelessly naïve.

The key to unlocking the double-voice in *The Conjure Woman*, which is difficult to identify at first, is hidden in the language itself. Chesnutt's text plays with the double meanings of a given signifier for subversive ends, much like the writing of his mentor George Washington Cable's in the 1880s,[20] but his most politically charged signifiers outwardly claim no apparent tie to their referent. As Dale E. Peterson points out, Chesnutt's naming of the white narrator (John) and the ex-slave (Julius) slyly references minstrelsy and slave folktales:

> Julius is one of the typical names white minstrels in blackface gave to the "end man" who springs the jokes at the expense of the interlocutor or "straight man"; John is one of the standard names for the black trickster who strives to outfox Massa in slave folklore. Any reader who catches these allusions will have a hard time deciding which of Chesnutt's rival narrators is the true trickster.[21]

For the reader who catches the allusion, the iconoclastic implication is that Chesnutt is calling out the nature of plantation tales for what they are (a blackface minstrelsy), opening up the possibility of reading Chesnutt's version of the plantation tale as a satire of the genre. If we map Chesnutt's "plantation tales" onto early minstrelsy, *The Conjure Woman* becomes a stage for the meeting of the (black) slave trickster and the (white blackface) stage trickster. In *Love and Theft*, Eric Lott situates early stages of minstrelsy at the intersection of "slave culture" and "earlier blackface stage characters," the latter referring to "the tradition of the harlequin, the clown, the burlesque tramp, and perhaps the 'blackman' of English folk drama."[22] As he explains, the two kinds of tricksters play separate roles in our cultural imagination: "Clowns and harlequins are butts of humor as well as devious producers of it; slave-tale tricksters are frequently (though not always) champions, heroes, backdoor victors for the weak over the strong.[E]arly minstrel figures overlapped with each tradition, tending more or less toward self-mockery on the one hand and subversion on the other" (22). Chesnutt's narrative is in fact written in a way that makes it possible to entertain the idea that the joke may really be on John ("the straight man"). This subversive reading gives license to deride John's smug sense of self-entitlement and disturbingly patronizing behavior toward Uncle Julius,[23] calling into question John's claim to moral authority.[24]

Despite the fact that he decidedly plays more the role of "Ole Massa" than the trickster role of "John" from African American folktales, "John" is not an entirely arbitrary name, given that the narrator's voice is always actually the writer's ventriloquism. Uncle Julius is not the only "true trickster" character who manipulates a seemingly foreclosed system, like the folkloric "John." After all, Chesnutt himself is the first black writer to get away with publishing a potentially explosive piece of satire with a publishing house he knew to be conservative,[25] under the guise of genteel plantation fiction, which was not known to be a vehicle for refuting racist ideology. Much like John in the "Ole Massa and John" folktales, whose ability to outsmart others seems to hinge on his talent for creating an illusion of reality as others want to perceive it,[26] Chesnutt succeeds in playing to his readers' fascination with plantation tales; he had previously noticed in his journal that "there was something romantic, to the Northern mind, about the southern negro, as commonplace and vulgar as he seems to us who come into contact with him every day."[27] In an oft-quoted passage from this journal, Chesnutt expressed the desire that his writing bring about "not so much the elevation of the colored people as the elevation of the whites."[28] Having concluded that "the subtle almost indefinable feeling of repulsion toward the negro, which is common to most Americans—and easily enough accounted for—cannot be stormed and taken by assault," he proposes another strategy, of "amusing them to lead them on imperceptibly, unconsciously step by step to the desired state of feeling." This is in keeping with the view of scholars who have seen Chesnutt's stories as being "deliberately contrived to condition or enlighten a white audience without forcing a direct emotional confrontation."[29]

Houghton Mifflin's target audience would most likely have identified with the white narrator throughout. Matthew R. Martin states that Chesnutt's stories "were read with apparently little distress by the audience which treasured [Thomas Nelson Page's] 'Marse Chan.'" Readers may have enjoyed Chesnutt's stories as trivial entertainment,[30] reaching a conclusion similar to Chesnutt's biographer that Uncle Julius was nothing more than a stock character, the conventional "petted servant" whose role is to reaffirm "his endearingly mock-devious nature."[31] To derive some pleasure in covertly mocking these readers is surely forgivable. After all, the willful blindness of the readers contributed to the historical condition of slavery, reflected in their craving for stories of a conveniently idealized present and a romantic past in the South.

The impact of Chesnutt's writing at this time may also rest on the fact that it does not actually leave such readers completely unilluminated. In the opening pages of "The Goophered Grapevine," when John first describes Patesville, a town loosely based on Fayetteville, he hints that he will have learned much more by the end of his narrative. The town, which at first seemed only to be defined by "calm that seemed almost sabbatic in its restfulness," is later to reveal that "underneath its somnolent exterior the deeper currents of life—love and hatred, joy and despair, ambition and avarice, faith and friendship—flowed not less steadily than in livelier attitudes" (4). This description not only signals the double structure in the narrative to follow but also sets up a shift that takes place later in the linear trajectory of the narrative, in which John will start to see something new by listening to Uncle Julius's stories. The general impression readers have may be that John does not change very much, but in "The Grey Wolf's Han't," we catch a glimpse of the significant shift in John's view of Uncle Julius's tales as he starts to perceive them as being more than simply amusement. Where he had been dismissive of the tales as "an ingenious fairytale" (159) in a previous story, John comes to describe them as "bearing the stamp of truth, faint, perhaps, but still discernible" (168): "Even the wildest was not without an element of pathos,—the tragedy, it might be, of the story itself; the shadow, never absent, of slavery and of ignorance; the sadness, always, of life as seen by the fading light of an old man's memory" (168).

What rarely seems crucial to scholarly discussions of *The Conjure Woman* is the foundational role played by John's wife, Annie, in Chesnutt's narrative, despite the fact that one could even say the entire premise of John's narrative is contingent on this character. It is Annie's "poor health" that prompts John to move to North Carolina in the first place; John would never have met Uncle Julius without Annie. John never depicts Annie in a negative light, noting her "sympathetic turn of mind" (40), skillful piano playing (103), and conscientiousness in "ploughing through a missionary report" (104). But although John readily concedes to Annie on these points, nothing suggests that he sees Annie as his intellectual equal. John's clear condescension manifests itself only once, very briefly, when he is exasperated over Annie's lack of interest in the study of philosophy "even when presented in the simplest and most lucid form" (164). This dismissive comment alone makes one wonder if, when Annie falls victim to unexplained depression, the nature of her "settled melancholy" (163) is not perhaps akin to that of another heroine in a contemporary work: Charlotte Perkins Gilman's *The Yellow Wallpaper* (1892). We will never know, because John's "frame story" overwrites Annie's point of view and renders her story a subordinate one. Like Uncle Julius, Annie is not given an opportunity to tell her side of the story. But Annie's actual influence on John is more significant than he might care to admit. His appreciation of Uncle Julius's stories as "bearing the stamp of truth" is in fact a direct echo of Annie's words: "The story *bears the stamp of truth*, if ever a story did,the story is true to nature, and might have happened half a hundred times, and no doubt did happen, in those horrid days before the war" (159, emphasis mine). Uncle Julius's ability to change the terms of reality through storytelling relies on Annie's capacity for empathy and proportionate indignation over cruelty and injustice in the system of slavery. In turn, Annie is able to exercise a kind of agency and authority usually reserved for John when she is moved to make decisions over household matters in a way that would help Uncle Julius, even if it runs counter to John's wishes.

This sympathetic character with the means to help the trickster is extremely important in considering the function of an "enabling" figure in Chesnutt's own life. The positive backing of William Dean Howells certainly seems to have contributed to Chesnutt's literary stature, just as Howells's opinion had done for the poet Paul Laurence Dunbar.[32] Yet Joseph R. McElrath Jr. notes that the *Atlantic*'s staff, and in particular its editor, Walter Hines Page, had already done much in first establishing

Chesnutt's literary stature. The *Atlantic* was long considered the apex of the literary world in the nineteenth century, and had printed Chesnutt's first story, "Dave's Neckliss," more than a decade before Howells's positive review of Chesnutt's works in 1901. The inclusion of Chesnutt's story in the *Atlantic* is significant, given that it was moving away from its rapid development into an increasingly elitist and exclusionist institution during the two decades leading up to Page's brief editorship there, which took place before he partnered with Doubleday to build his own firm.[33] Page played a crucial mediating role in the publication of *The Conjure Woman* by Houghton Mifflin, which housed the *Atlantic*. While Chesnutt had consulted George Washington Cable about his writing earlier in his career, it was to Page that he expressed the fundamental challenge of writing in dialect:

> Speaking of dialect, it is almost a despairing task to write it. What to do with the troublesome *r*, and the obvious inconsistency of leaving it out where it would be in good English, and putting it in where correct speech would leave it out, how to express such words as "here" and "hear" and "Year" and "other" and "another," "either" and "neither," and so on, is a "'stractin'" task. The fact is, of course, that there is no such thing as Negro dialect; that what we call by that name is the attempt to express, with such a degree of phonetic correctness as to suggest the sound, English pronounced as an ignorant old southern Negro would be supposed to speak it, and at the same time to preserve a sufficient approximation to the correct spelling to make it easy reading. . . . I shall be glad to receive any suggestions in the matter of the dialect or anything else.[34]

As it might be surmised from the way in which Chesnutt refers to the task of writing in dialect, as "a 'stractin' task," Page was originally from North Carolina. This was a fact that initially surprised Chesnutt, who assumed "as nine people out of ten would offhand," that an editor of the *Atlantic* was "of course, a New Englander by birth and breeding."[35]

During his formative years, Page had travelled extensively both in his own country and in Europe, which has been described as "an almost unprecedented thing for a Southern youth of that day."[36] He had returned to North Carolina in the early 1880s with a broadened intellectual outlook that formed his political vision for the "New South," of which he became a leading spokesman. He was a proponent of free universal education for all as a means to rehabilitate the South, and his vision did not exclude African Americans. He criticized "the silent unwillingness of white men to tax themselves to educate the Negro, the instinctive denial to the Negro of any real standing in the most important matters of life," and advocated educational opportunities for black children by saying that "training to economic independence is the only true emancipation": "As slavery and war and an isolated life arrested their development and held them in a fixed social condition, so the proper training of them to helpful occupations will release them to usefulness in a democracy."[37]

It was the insurmountable difficulty Page encountered in attempting to bring change to North Carolina that forced him, as Burton J. Hendricks mentions in his Pulitzer Prize–winning biography of Page, to "forego his hope of playing a part in rescuing his state from the disasters of the Civil War."[38] Page's active literary career in Boston and New York, then, was a result of his utter disappointment with the South, which he left in 1885, having "cast off the shackles of provinciality for the freedom of Cosmopolitanism." North Carolina was to stay in the grip of what Page himself had seen as a "mummified aristocracy[which] was driving the best talent and initiative from the state" (46). Page seems to have thrived in that realm defined by cosmopolitanism in the North, where his ambitions and conduct would eventually lead him to an ambassadorship in the Court of St. James in 1916 under the Woodrow Wilson administration.

Chesnutt was one among many writers whom Page had encouraged in the course of his publishing career, a roster that gives us a hint of what his vision in politics might have been. During his time at the *Atlantic*, Page acquired contributions from public figures like Frederick Jackson Turner, E. L. Godkin, Woodrow Wilson, Theodore Roosevelt, and James Bryce, while he also published works by women writers like Ellen Glasgow and Mary Johnston. He accepted Theodor Dreiser's *Sister Carrie* for publication, although apparently his authority as a partner at Doubleday, Page was not enough when he met strong opposition from Mrs. Doubleday. However limited his role may seem from our current vantage point, Page was behind the reprint of Booker T. Washington's *Up from Slavery*, making it accessible to a larger audience;[39] Page was also behind the publication of Joel Chandler Harris's Uncle Remus tales, the commercial success of which created the market for the publication of plantation fiction by Charles Chesnutt.

Even though the commercial failure of Chesnutt's second book, *The Marrow of Tradition*, closed the doors of Houghton Mifflin on Chesnutt, Page went on to publish Chesnutt's *The Colonel's Dream* (1905) from his own firm, Doubleday, Page. A recurring notion in Page's collection of essays on the publishing industry that same year, *A Publisher's Confession* (1905), is the idea that "publishing as publishing" was something other than moneymaking, which can be done through sales of educational textbooks, subscription books, and magazines.[40] He argued that "publishing houses in the United States conducted as dignified institutions" are run "with as little degrading commercialism as the old houses whose history has become a part of English literature" (74). Not simply "a mere job done under contract, a commercial job and nothing more," publishing involves more than printing and advertising to sell a book:[41]

> For my part, while I am as glad as Podunk, Exploitem & Company to have novels that will sell 100,000 copies, provided they give clean and decent amusement, I take no permanent interest in anything that comes this month and goes the next; nor does any serious man. My wish and aim is to become a helpful partner of some of the men and women of my generation who can, by their writings, lay the great democracy that we all serve under obligations to them for a new impulse. By serving them, I, too, serve my country and my time. And when I say that this is my aim and wish, I could say with equal truth that it is the aim and wish of every other real publisher. (174–75)

My discussion of the relationship between Charles Chesnutt and Walter Hines Page, which I have sketched out, is not meant to challenge the fact that black writers and white editors or publishers have often had a vexed history throughout the twentieth century, nor is it meant to deny that race has been exploited by white editors and publishers time and again. Through careful textual analysis and archival work, John K. Young in *Black Writers, White Publishers: Marketplace Politics in Twentieth-Century African American Literature* demonstrates how important changes had to be made in major texts by African American writers in order to meet the demands of publishing houses like Boni and Liveright (Jean Toomer), Knopf (Nella Larsen and Toni Morrison), and Lippincott (Zora Neale Hurston), and at times to meet the marketing needs of white institutions like Book of the Month Club (Richard Wright).[42] As he writes, the white publisher–black author relationship is a part of the problematic cultural dynamic shaping the publishing industry at large: "The predominantly white publishing industry reflects and often reinforces the racial divide that has always defined American society, representing 'blackness' as a one-dimensional cultural experience."[43] Young may be right that a productive literary interracial relationship like that of Ralph Ellison and Albert Erskine at Random House was rare. I would argue, however, that it is precisely because it is rare that these cross-cultural collaborations deserve our attention. The very fact that such an undertaking was rare tells us as much about the conflicted interracial history of African American writers and their white editors and publishers.

Silence as Signifying: Sui Sin Far's Short Stories and William Hayes Ward

On September 21, 1896, the *Montreal Daily Star* printed a letter to its editors, "A Plea for the Chinaman: A Correspondent's Argument in His Favor," signed by "E. E." The letter was written in response to the debates in the Canadian Parliament over whether to raise the amount of "head tax" imposed on each Chinese person seeking entry into Canada from ten dollars to five hundred dollars.[44] In making an argument against this law,[45] the letter references the U.S. Chinese Exclusion Act, just renewed in 1892. In doing so, "E. E." commented, it "looks as if it was got up for the sole purpose of giving unprincipled lawyers and corrupt Government officers a chance to do some boodling."[46] We know that "E. E." stood for Edith (Maude) Eaton, the British-born Canadian émigré writer otherwise known as Sui Sin Far, whom we have come to know as the first writer of Asian descent to publish in North America.[47] Two widely known short stories by Sui Sin Far were counter-"boodling" narratives reminiscent of Bret Harte's maligned satire "Plain Language from Truthful James" (1870), in which two miners collude to cheat the "heathen Chinee" in a card game, only to have him turn the tables and best them both by holding spare cards in his inside sleeves and winning at a game they thought he did not understand. In "Tian Shan's Kindred Spirit," a Chinese outlaw character wanted for his adventurous border crossings has eluded customs officers—quoting Harte's "Truthful James"—"by ways that are dark and tricks that are vain." "The Smuggling of Tie Co" presents Jack Fabian, who makes a business out of contrabanding the Chinese from Canada into the United States. Sui Sin Far herself may have engaged in border-crossing tricksterism in real life, with her numerous trips between the United States and Canada, using her English name and Anglo appearance.[48] The most difficult border crossing was the gulf between the Chinese in the United States, whom she wrote about, and her white audience. For this, she needed the help of a Jack Fabian or two. Sui Sin Far's "In the Land of the Free," published in the *Independent*, held up the Chinese Exclusion Act as a failure of the United States to measure up to its ideals of egalitarian liberal democracy.

The story opens in San Francisco with the arrival of a ship from China, the *Eastern Queen*. A young Chinese woman aboard the ship speaks to her two-year-old son: "See, Little One—the Hills in the morning sun.

There is thy home for years to come. It is very beautiful and thou wilt be very happy here." Finally set free from family obligations that had kept her in China long after the birth of her son, Lae Choo is returning to San Francisco, where her husband, a Chinese merchant, will see his son for the very first time. America awaits in all its legendary glory, and that morning sunshine seems to promise a bright future with exciting new possibilities. The story quickly dispels any such notion, beginning with a moment when the customs officers, who seemed friendly at first, refuse to grant entry to the child because he was not born in the United States. The child is taken away from the parents and placed under federal custody until the officers can obtain clearance from Washington. The parents are initially led to believe that the child will likely be returned to them the following day, but several months go by without the case getting reviewed. All seems hopeless until a white lawyer arrives on the scene, offering to negotiate with the officials in Washington. This is no easy deus ex machina, however, for the "negotiation" actually means bribery, on top of which the lawyer will help only if they can come up with five hundred dollars for his services. The father, Hom Hing, does not have the money, but when the mother understands the situation, she thinks of handing over her jewelry (her bracelet, jade earrings, gold buttons, hair pins, comb of pearl, and rings), and the problem seems to be finally solved. The lawyer delivers on his promise to get the child back, but the final twist is that when the mother goes to take her son home, falling on her knees and stretching out her arms, the child tries to shoo her away, hiding behind the skirt of the white woman who took care of the children at the missions.

It is difficult to read the title and the opening scene for the second time without feeling a sense of irony. Having seen what the mother would have to go through after her arrival, her words in the opening scene, "it is very beautiful and thou wilt be very happy here," would ring hollow; "here is thy home for years to come" is no longer such an attractive prospect. The "morning on the hills" is also "mourning on the hills." The experience of encountering what one first thought was a positive to be completely drained of its meaning the second time around, mimetically reproduces the disillusionment of the Chinese immigrants who found themselves to be objects of exclusion. This is true of the pattern of the story itself, which is a series of repeated disappointments following a hopeful moment. Similarly, the title's reference to the heightened moment in the national anthem when the music swells up as the notes climb higher and a crescendo leads up to the coda, will end there; the title does not include the words that complete the anthem, "and the home of the brave." Giving meaning to silence is particularly important because the exclusionary status of Asian Americans, against whom the American citizenship had coalesced, had meant the silencing of their voice, as King-Kok Cheung argued in *Articulate Silences* (1993). It matters here that Sui Sin Far makes use of silence as the very means with which to establish a critical standpoint.

But how is it that the reader is able to understand what Lae Choo was saying to her baby aboard the ship, in the first place? It is clear from the other parts of the story that the Chinese mother's English is limited. When the customs officers try to take the child from her husband Hom Hing's arms, she says, "No, you not take him; he my son too."[49] The next time she speaks in English is to the lawyer, when she says, "You are a hundred man good!" (507); upon learning that his services require a fee that Hom Hing does not have, we hear her say, "You not one hundred man good; you just common white man." Lae Choo's voice becomes louder as the narrative moves along, and we hear her speak the longest when the lawyer starts to leave and she stops him, saying, "If Hom Hing not can give you five hundred dollars—I give you five hundred dollars—I give you perhaps what more that much.See, my jade earrings—my gold buttons—my hairpins—my comb of pearl and my rings—one, two, three, four, five rings; very good—very good—all same much money. I give them all to you. You take and bring me paper for my Little One" (508). As though it were a settled matter, the story opens with a bilingual narrator who translates Lae Choo's Chinese, using "thou" and "thy" as pronouns indicating foreignness without compromising her integrity. Conversations in Chinese between Lae Choo and Hom Hing are made accessible to a non-Chinese-speaking reader as well, establishing the mother as a full person while she is speaking in Chinese. The empathy created in that first half of the story makes it easier to ignore her broken English and maintain our empathy. Lae Choo's broken English becomes important, as it is the very struggle in her effort to communicate with the lawyer in a language that is foreign to her that adds to the urgency of the scene.

Evelyn Nien-ming Ch'ien identifies the rhetorical strategy in the work of contemporary writers who blend more than one language with English in their writing, such as Paul Beatty, Irvine Welsh, Derek Walcott, Li-Young Lee, Junot Díaz, and Lois Ann Yamanaka, each inflected by the vernacular of a particular diasporic community. "Weird-English writers," as she calls them, "denormalize English out of resistance to it, and form their own language by combining English with their original language.[F]or weird-English writers, the composition of weird English is an active way of *takin' the community back*" (6). She argues that as a philosophical and linguistic entity, the vernacular transcription has "a built-in self-consciousness of its political, social, and metaphorical implications, as well as aesthetic value." As such, it belongs as a subset of—and an innovation in the category of—experimental English. While the plot has the appearance of moving from inclusion to exclusion of Lae Choo, clinched by the refusal of her child to recognize his mother, the story itself is from the outset based on translation as an inclusive gesture into a world that had excluded the reader because of language, making new identification possible.

Some readers of the *Independent* would have been familiar with Sui Sin Far's autobiographical essay "Leaves from the Mental Portfolio of an Eurasian," which had appeared earlier that year. "Leaves" is a well-crafted narrative that avoids antagonizing potentially sympathetic white readers of the *Independent*. The oval portrait photo of Sui Sin Far above the text showed her to have Anglo features, as Sui Sin Far resembled her British father more than her Chinese mother. Annette White-Parks notes that her European features contained within the standard frame of Victorian portraits would have suggested to a largely white audience that she was "a 'safe ethnic'—one who looked white"—before moving on to identify the appeal of conquered hardship as a familiar rhetoric to that audience, who had "overcome difficulties to 'pull herself up by the bootstraps,' as the American dream said she would" (199). While the narrative about her life depicts her encounters with racist behavior of others that had damaged her feelings throughout her life, instances of truly abhorrent racist behavior happen in her childhood in Britain and in French Canada, or are witnessed in Jamaica, where she lived briefly as a journalist. A fairly large section of "Leaves" narrates her experiences in the United States as an adult, but the essay consistently portrays white people in favorable light. Mr. K., her employer in a town in the Midwest who says at a gathering that he cannot reconcile himself with the thought that "the Chinese are humans like themselves," is ultimately praised as "a conscientious Christian man" with "moral courage" because he apologizes to her once she tells him that she is Chinese, owning up to the fact that his prejudice came from his ignorance.[50] "Leaves" finds a way to redeem "white men, and women . . . who are too proud to mate with those who have Chinese blood in their veins," concluding that "I think it a great honor to be distinguished by the friendship of such" (131). When she narrates a story about a Eurasian girl who got engaged to a white man, despite the fact that his extreme persistence actually borders on stalking in present-day terms (she refused his proposal nine times), in their dialogue he comes across to us as a benevolent person while the Eurasian girl sounds self-centered and unreasonable. She encounters people in the literary world who annoyingly advise her to play up the exoticism of her ethnicity, suggesting that she "dress in Chinese costume, carry a fan in [her] hand, wear a pair of scarlet beaded slippers, live in New York, and come of high birth," going around chanting bogus Confucius sayings. She calls them "funny people," seemingly more amused than offended by them (133). In the course of telling captivating stories about her life across continents and in different cities, she subtly guides readers toward the kind of civil behavior that wins her admiration and praise, while discouraging them from various kinds of racist behavior.

"Leaves" posits the working-class Chinese immigrant at the margins of its narrative, as figures that appear near the beginning and toward the end, another recognizable configuration for her readers. The stationary figures establish the centrality of the bourgeois "Eurasian" subjectivity formed in transnational mobility; it is against these working-class global migrants, for whom border crossings have become difficult, that a cosmopolitan global subject emerges. These figures actually become central to the narrative despite their marginal status in narrative representation, in the sense that Sui Sin Far ultimately embraces them as people with whom she identifies and whom she considers worth fighting for. When she encounters Chinese immigrants in Hudson City, New York, for the first time, she perceives them as the *other*: "The two men within the store are uncouth specimens of their race, drest in working blouses and pantaloons with queues hanging down their backs. I recoil with a sense of shock. 'Oh, Charlie,' I cry, 'Are we like that?'" (126). Sui Sin Far and her brother are taunted by the neighborhood children immediately afterward, who call them "Chinky, Chinky, Chinaman, yellow-face, pig-tail, rat-eater." To this she screams back defiantly, "I'd rather be Chinese than anything else in the world," and gets into a fight with the children: "they tear my clothes, they scratch my face, and all but lame my brother; but the white blood in our veins fights valiantly for the Chinese half of us. When it is all over, exhausted and bedraggled, we crawl home, and report to our mother that we have 'won the battle.'" Scholars have noted that Sin Far attributes greater valor and passion to "white blood,"[51] and I am inclined to extend that criticism to say that the notion of identity situated in the realm of biological essentialism rather than that of performativity is itself problematic. But this could also be read as another strategy to sustain the sympathy of her white readers at an emblematic moment. The voiceless working-class immigrant appears on the scene once again as her essay draws to a close: "a Chinese vegetable gardener's cart came rumbling along. The Chinaman was a jolly-looking individual in blue cotton blouse and pantaloons, his rakish looking hat being kept in place by a long queue which was pulled upward from his neck and wound around it" (132). Here, Sui Sin Far depicts a Eurasian girl who has become friends with the narrator, telling her white fiancé that she was planning on giving a Chinese party every month, inviting all classes of Chinese people: "As there are very few aristocratic Chinese in this city, I shall fill up with the laundrymen and vegetable farmers. I don't believe in being exclusive in democratic America, do you?"

More than any other literary outlet, scholars have so far focused on Sui Sin Far's politics in the short stories published in the 1890s in a Californian journal called the *Land of Sunshine* ("Ku Yum," "A Chinese Feud," "The Chinese Woman in America," "Sweet Sin," "The Sing-Song Woman," "Lin John," "The Story of Tin-A," "The Smuggling of Tie Co," and "O Yam—A Sketch"). This is perhaps appropriate, for as Mike Davis has noted, its editor, Charles Fletcher Lummis, was a crucial figure in creating a comprehensive fiction of Southern California as "the promised land of a millenarian Anglo-Saxon racial odyssey," which had enormous impact on images reproduced by Hollywood and shaped the "ersatz landscapes of suburban Southern California"; he was indeed an important figure who left a "legacy" of many writers, antiquarians, and publicists at the turn of the twentieth century, who "inserted a Mediterraneanized idyll of New England life into the perfumed ruins of an innocent but inferior 'Spanish' culture."[52] Dominika Ferens characterizes the *Land of Sunshine* under Lummis's editorship to have been a forum for the Euro-American elite on the West Coast, subsidized by entrepreneurs for whom the ethnography of Native Americans and local Chinese, accurate or otherwise, conveniently worked as "local color" to cover up the presence of the white working class in California.[53]

Lummis makes an appearance in "Leaves" as "the editor of the magazine who took my first Chinese stories," portrayed in a positive light: "He and his wife gave me a warm welcome to their ranch. They are broadminded people, whose interest in me is sincere and intelligent, not affected and vulgar." But in reality, what his journal had to offer was also limited. According to Ferens, Lummis himself had no special interest in the Chinese as an ethnic group, nor did he believe they could or should be American citizens. Martha J. Cutter writes that the *Land of Sunshine* was predisposed to cultural dictates that held skewed notions about Asian Americans, and its fiction often created and reinforced racist stereotypes about the Chinese that Sui Sin Far had to contest through her own stories. Her short stories included Chinese characters whose speech was not Standard English, but it was also not the foolish dialect represented elsewhere in the journal as "authentic speech" of the Chinese in the United States. In the short story "O Yam," for instance, the Chinese speaker is also an "honorable, loving, trustworthy man." The *Land of Sunshine*'s limitations in offering proper representation of Asian Americans are a function of its targeted audience.

The *Independent*, which published Sui Sin Far's stories from 1909 to 1913, during the vibrant late period of her writing career, provided an outlet that allowed her short stories to be more visibly political than many of her other short stories while giving her a chance to address a national audience. Initially established in 1848 by three Congregational ministers, the *Independent* had been a prominent antislavery voice during the nineteenth century and had supported the women's suffrage movement from the beginning. Seeing itself as the "Christian conscience of the North," the *Independent* believed in demanding "equality and treatment for every citizen of whatever race or color."[54] The journal had expressed its vociferous opposition to the Chinese Exclusion Act throughout the 1880s and 1890s, calling the law "an abomination" and a "disgrace."[55] William Hayes Ward, who became their editor in chief in 1896, came from an old New England family in Abington, Massachusetts. With a grandfather and a father who were both ministers, Ward aspired at one point was to go into the Congregational ministry, and after his education at Amherst College he briefly attended Yale Divinity School and graduated from Andover Theological Seminary in 1859. Although the *Independent* was no longer an explicitly religious journal under Ward's editorship, Christian ideals still influenced the way Ward saw his work: "It is not worthwhile to be an editor or publisher just to make money; leave that to small souls. Money can wisely be lost for a cause."[56] Thus on October 17, 1901, with the Chinese Exclusion Act soon to be extended for the second time, and this time permanently, the *Independent* ran an editorial in which it stated that "we have opposed these laws from the beginning, and believe they ought not to be extended over another term of years."

However, the *Independent* was caught in a dilemma during the 1900s as it became a lively forum for social progressives, which required an adjustment of the journal's traditionally vociferous stance against the Chinese Exclusion Act. Jacob Riis and social economists like John R. Commons, among others who started contributing to the *Independent*, generally held anti-Chinese views, which were inseparable from the nativist logic of the movement. As Sean McCann explains: "American hostility [toward the Chinese] was closely associated with the reformist energies that characterized the political atmosphere of the late nineteenth and early twentieth centuries. From the first attacks on Chinese workers in the 1850s, the key supporters of Chinese exclusion had been the nascent forces of organized labor, who blamed the Chinese for keeping wages low and for undermining worker solidarity. At the core of the era's nativist belief was the notion that 'all ethnic strangers were a strain on the nation's social health.'"[57] Taking a hard stand against the Chinese Exclusion Act posed a problem in that the gesture could be seen as an endorsement for the moneyed class that relied on the presence of cheap Chinese labor.

As we might suspect from his inclusion of Sui Sin Far's stories, Ward still found ways of contesting prejudiced views against the Chinese without directly addressing the Chinese Exclusion Act. During the 1900s, the *Independent* refrained from making its own commentary but declared itself a journal that strove to "inform its readers of the strength even of policies which it did not approve."[58] In 1902, it printed Senator Boies Penrose's article in favor of renewing the Chinese Exclusion Act, though not necessarily committing to Penrose's view that "we must see to it that the line is drawn more narrowly than ever before against paupers, idiots, convicts, laborers under contract, aliens who are diseased, and all others who may contaminate or weaken the body social or the body politic.We remain lovers of liberty still; but we can no longer afford to be regarded merely as an 'Asylum for the Oppressed.'"[59] At the same time, Ward hired a translator to deliver a first-person account of a Chinese resident, which gave him a chance to argue back: "It was the jealousy of laboring men of other nationalities—especially the Irish—that raised all the outcry against the Chinese. No one would hire an Irishman, German, Englishman or Italian when he could get a Chinese because our countrymen are so much more honest, industrious, steady, sober and painstaking. The Chinese were persecuted, not for their vices, but for their virtues. There never was any honesty in the pretended fear of leprosy or in the cheap Chinese scare, and the persecution continues still, because Americans make a mere practice of loving justice. They are all for money making, and they want to be on the strongest side always."[60]

To be sure, Ward's inclusion of countervailing voices set against the social progressives may also have come from his inclination toward conservative views on political economy, as expressed toward the end of his editorship, in the November 7, 1912, issue:

> I presume I should be expected to mention . . . industrial injustice and slavery. We hear much of it, and some of it there is; but I confess that I have not been able to see that the radical remedy which

> socialism offers would not create more complete monopoly and greater injustice and tyranny. Certainly great combinations of capital must be controlled that labor may have its rights, and I would have *The Independent* very watchful against such recurring evils; but I do not yet see it clear that property is robbery. (1039)

Ward's reluctance to condemn different forms of injustice under industrial capitalism other than corporate monopoly, as well as his resistance toward the notion that "property is robbery," suggest that his support of the labor movement and its rights only extends to the degree that it provides an appropriately strong counterbalance to forces of capital. It is within that framework that the *Independent* under Ward claimed to have supported "every movement for the betterment of the conditions of labor." His successor, Hamilton Holt, wrote that Ward had "a secret liking, if not for the Socialists, at least for socialism.But he had no patience with the socialist claim that the poor are growing poorer. 'Look about you in any town or city,' said he, 'and the hundreds of prosperous and decent homes of the workers belie that idea.'"[61] Ward's view is in line with abolitionist critique of slavery, which at times entailed a defense of wage labor. Citing the work done by historians of free market ideology like David Brion Davis and Eric Foner, Jeffrey Sklansky explains that "in identifying the oppressive character of slavery with the extra-economic compulsion of labor by means of law and violence, leading abolitionists implicitly and often explicitly equated freedom as well as class harmony with contractual relations between labor and capital."[62]

Through its editorials, the *Independent* also urged readers to consider issues in terms of global politics and foreign policy rather than domestic commercial interests. In 1904, as the Russo-Japanese War began, they warned readers that the real "Yellow Peril" was the Japanese imperialist expansion, which had led to Japan's victory in a war against China in 1895: "That there will be any Yellow Peril through China invading the West, as the Huns once invaded Europe, is past belief. Those days are gone. A different civilization prevails and will prevail."[63] Ward himself was an enthusiastic supporter of U.S. expansion, and the *Independent* supported "the annexation of San Domingo under President Grant and tho that failed it has since seen Samoa, Guam, Porto [*sic*] Rico, the Philippines and Hawaii brought under our beneficient flag."[64] His hopes for "success in our island possessions" were in no way ironic. From his article on Puerto Rico written in 1899, it is clear that he genuinely believed that the United States was there to help achieve a higher quality of life for the people in Puerto Rico. He noted the U.S. order of a year's suspension of the summary foreclosure of mortgages on agricultural property, for instance, while protesting against the continuation of Spanish tariffs on imported goods, and he seems certain that "we Americans will introduce better schools." I realize the danger of overlooking the potentially imperialistic nature of this statement. Yet at this point in history, when in the Caribbean no U.S. effort has been made to restore the library (in Antigua) decades after the publication of Jamaica Kincaid's *A Small Place* to right the wrong of British imperialism in the past, and when the news of U.S. drone air strikes destroying schools in other parts of the world like Yemen now reaches us on a regular basis, Ward's vision of U.S. leadership in the world is not easy to dismiss.

2 / The Making of the Cosmopolitan Subject

Writing from New York in the early 1990s, in recollection of San Francisco at the beginning of her career, Jessica Hagedorn describes strong new voices in the Bay Area emerging at what she calls "a glorious and heady time." Talented writers from previously marginalized social groups had begun to bring change to the cultural landscape in the late 1960s and early 1970s: "Defiant, naive, passionate, we are sprouting up all over the Bay Area—artists of color who write, perform, and collaborate with each other, borders be damned."[1] This animated collaboration among artists of color indeed opened up wide possibilities for creative expression, but through a discussion of Hagedorn's own early writing, I argue in this chapter that one extraordinary cross-cultural collaboration happened between writers and their innovative publishers, who envisioned and established new literary platforms that reached across boundaries of race and gender to include Asian American writing for the first time in U.S. cultural history. Poets themselves, these innovators were setting up their own publishing houses and literary journals, holding poetry readings, securing a solid foundation upon which a new generation of artists could thrive at a time when the mainstream publishing industry mostly continued to uphold purported standards that effectively sealed off ethnic/racial minorities and women from publishing their works. While the historical reality of San Francisco had often been a harsh one for ethnic and racial minorities, this new imagined community in San Francisco carved out new space where boundary crossing was possible, and where the figure of the new cosmopolitan Asian American subject could be dreamt and written into being.

A major port of entry to the United States, San Francisco was no exception to the historical propensity of American cities to display hostile expressions of anti-Asian sentiment.[2] In 1888, the city took the Filipino poet Jose Rizal by bitter surprise upon his arrival in the United States when he found himself barred entry and detained on Angel Island in San Francisco Bay, along with 642 Chinese passengers, and placed under quarantine.[3] The glittering promise of economic prosperity dissipated in a matter of years for Chinese miners who arrived during the gold rush, but the lure of the "Gold Mountain" had still drawn 322,000 Chinese people through the San Francisco Custom House over the course of three decades, from 1852 to the passing of the Chinese Exclusion Act in 1882.[4] The Angel Island Poems of Chinese detainees held in the barracks from 1910 to 1940 often revolved around the idea of the "jail cell" or "prison" as a heightened expression of the reality of discriminatory policies that awaited them in the United States,[5] and by the 1970s, Frank Chin saw San Francisco as a city that "worked hard to build a racist kennel."[6] Its urban planners were also ruthless in tearing down homes in these segregated ethnic urban enclaves. During the decades following World War II, as with major cities across the nation, many of San Francisco's minority neighborhoods were demolished to make way for mass-scale city redevelopment.[7] Most visibly, this aggression culminated in the devastating destruction of the last standing symbolic remnant of Manilatown, I-Hotel, a low-income single-room-occupancy residence that was home to many elderly Filipino Americans. This was the city where Hagedorn arrived as a teenager in 1964, and her early years as a poet roughly overlapped the decade-long eviction proceedings leading up to the forced evictions that started on August 4, 1977, followed by the physical destruction of the I-Hotel building in 1979.

At the same time, San Francisco was also strikingly unique for its capacity to nurture and embrace politics and aesthetics formed in marginality, shaped as it was by multiple countercultural forces. Independent of the publishing marketplace dominated by large publishing houses along the East Coast, and distinct from the mass culture industry of Los Angeles, San Francisco and the Greater Bay Area in the late 1960s was to become a space of heightened resistance for avant-garde poetry, the Black Arts movement, the emerging Chicano/Latino literary movement, and Second Wave/Third World feminism. It was here that many Asian American publications started, from the Chinese-language newspaper the *Oriental* (1827–) to journals in English like *Pacific Citizen* (1929–) founded by the oldest and largest Asian Pacific Association, the Japanese-American Citizens' League; *AION* (1970–71), the first Asian American literary journal, was founded by the Japanese American poets Janice Mirikitani and Francis Oka. Civil rights–inspired activism revolving around the I-Hotel resulted in the formation of the Kearney Street Workshop, the first Asian American multidisciplinary nonprofit organization for the arts to create its own press. The University of California, Berkeley, was alma mater to Frank Chin, Shawn Wong, Jeffrey Paul Chan, and Lawson Fusao Inada, the four editors of the touchstone Asian American anthology, *AIIIEEEEE!: An Anthology of Asian American Writers* (1974). Still, the important cultural alliances in literary production that took place in the San Francisco area between writers, editors, and publishers often did not form exclusively along ethnic/racial borders. Rather, many new publications featuring Asian American writing were distinctively multicultural, taking shape in response to the overwhelming need to cultivate a new mode of literary production and dissemination.

This chapter explores multiple ways in which Asian American writers came in contact with San Francisco's variegated cultural front, negotiating and creating interweaving cultural alliances as each worked out imagined solutions to ongoing social and political tension. The first section of this chapter details the cross-cultural collaborations between Jessica Hagedorn and the various editors who supported her early career, moving beyond the standard accounts of Hagedorn's early development within the contemporary literary field, in which the San Francisco Renaissance poet Kenneth Rexroth (1905–1982) has traditionally been the one key literary figure recognized for introducing her to the (white) San Francisco literary scene.[8]

To be sure, Rexroth's stature and influence was indeed significant, enough to get Hagedorn's poems published in *Four Young Women: Poems* (1973) from McGraw-Hill, only two years after William Morrow had published Lawson Inada's *Before the War: Poems as They Happened*, long seen as the first stand-alone collection of poems by an Asian American poet.[9] Rexroth was very much aware of the difficulty young poets faced in finding a place to publish their works, especially if they were women and/or minorities:

> Certain kinds of poetry by members of racial minorities in the United States find ready publication. A stereotype is growing up as rigid as that of the old minstrel show. Protest, revolt are fine, but black, brown and yellow people are human beings and live human lives with human problems and human glories and do something else besides protest even if that's all the guilty dominant race wants to hear.[10]

Four Young Women was to inaugurate Rexroth's new poetry series, featuring the best of poetry that brought change to the "provincial" and "conventional" character of the prevailing poetry publishing scene, which Rexroth claimed had been dominated by "the theories of the long-bygone New Criticism and the examples of English baroque verse and the American self-styled Reactionary Generation" (ix). San Francisco, for that matter, had long attracted poets from other parts of the nation who wanted to escape "the fractional, ultimately commercial, pressures of the East" and "the infighting of the New York literary cocktail parties."[11] This contributed to San Francisco's cosmopolitanism, in his view, with its closer cultural contact with London and Paris than New York: "Young poets in San Francisco were much more aware of the New Romantics, Apocalyptics, and libertarians in wartime London, and the poets of the Resistance in France, than most writers in New York."[12]

Instead of continuing to direct the spotlight on Kenneth Rexroth, this chapter sheds new light on the cross-cultural collaborations of the San Francisco literary scene in the first section, by turning to publishers of new small literary presses whose significant role in Hagedorn's early career has been eclipsed by Rexroth's presence. Many from this new generation of exciting poets and artists, including Hagedorn, were greatly aided by poets like Ishmael Reed (Yardbird Press), Alta (Shameless Hussy Press), and Stephen Vincent (Momo's Press), who each created dynamic multicultural literary platforms where no such establishment had existed. When Rexroth introduced Hagedorn to a large (white) audience for the first time in *Four Young Women*, he announced, "as a premium, one of the four is a member of the Third World." Progressive as this may have been at the time, this statement gives an impression that the "Third World" is a monolithic realm, such that one of the four young poets was sufficient as far as representation went, as opposed to the other three white female poets (Carol Tinker, Barbara Szerlip, and Alice Karle), whose voices were individually worthy of attention. By contrast, a wide range of voices from the "Third World" were introduced in *Third World Women* (1972), the first anthology for women writers of color in U.S. literary history. *Third World Women* included Hagedorn's one-act play *Chiquita Banana* (based on Carmen Miranda) and was published a year prior to Rexroth's *Four Young Women*. The anthology was published by Third World Communications Collective, a small literary press that Hagedorn edited for, created by poets including Ntozake Shange, Janice Mirikitani, and Nina Serrano. Although Yardbird Press, Shameless Hussy Press, Momo's Press, and Third World Women's Collective were each clearly defined by their own particular identity politics and aesthetic vision, they were all pioneering enterprises that brought multiculturalism into being. As Kobena Mercer has pointed out, "solidarity [in multiculturalism] does not mean that everyone thinks the same way[;] it begins when people have the confidence to disagree over issues of fundamental importance precisely because they 'care' about constructing common ground."[13] In practice, the material aspect of such "common ground" must begin by establishing a medium like a publishing house that can then create new alternative literary space for those who had theretofore been barred entry.

How do we assess the value of these cross-cultural collaborations? Hagedorn herself offers a critical perspective on this imagined community in her literary work, one that allows us to read cross-cultural collaborations against the grain—less as utopian moments than as occasions for exploitation. Hagedorn's 1981 novella "Pet Food" provides a harsh critique of multiculturalism in the context of emerging structures of globalization and transnational capitalism. Unlike neoconservative critiques often launched at multiculturalism, which refuse to recognize the legitimacy of anything other than the Euro-American–centric model of historiography,[14] Hagedorn's work raises concern for minorities who are further disenfranchised by a focus on a handful of privileged and successful minorities whose presence actually participates in and reinforces the exploitative structure of late capitalism. An uncritical celebration of multiculturalism is, in this sense, like a birthday party where the guest of honor is absent, or even dead.

In fact, at a culminating moment of Hagedorn's novella, a teenage Filipino American musician lies dead in the shower as his birthday party goes on without him. Unbeknownst to his guests, he had overdosed on a birthday gift from the novella's Filipino American protagonist. As it happens, the birthday party is also meant to celebrate the completion of the protagonist's manuscript, and thus it is a dual celebration for the "birth of the Asian American artist"—one birth biological, the other symbolic. The portrayal of the invited guests includes a satirical treatment of Kenneth Rexroth and his entourage[15] carrying on merrily, oblivious to the fact that what is in order is actually mourning rather than a celebration. The writerly Asian American subject supposedly celebrated here overwrites another kind of Asian American subjectivity found in earlier narratives of Asian immigrants, erasing them from cultural memory and thus preparing the way for the privileged cosmopolitan subject. Moreover, the celebrated manuscript completed by Hagedorn's protagonist is not a collection of poems but a script for a Broadway musical financed by transnational capital. Within the context of globalization, now running the postindustrial economy, creative expression can be reduced to a cultural commodity expected to create returns on shareholder investments and capital gains. Commodification and commercialization of art sustains the exploitative economic structure of globalization, and without intending to, the artist participates in a globalized postindustrial economy that shapes the severe living conditions of those who continue to toil in what Giorgio Agamben calls "zones of indistinction,"[16] many among them Asian, inside and outside of the United States.

The arrival of the cosmopolitan writerly subject can certainly threaten to prematurely dislodge the critical imperative of early multiculturalism and minority discourse; the working-class immigrant can all too easily be marginalized once again, a dark double to be resubjugated as the subaltern and unduly banished to outmodedness, abjection, and silence. As I suggest toward the end of this chapter, however, yet another important act of epistemological violence occurs with the erasure of those who are involved in the collaborative process that goes into the material production of this very critique in the form of publication. The novella itself does not attest to the significant labor of someone other than the writer that goes into editing the manuscript, finding artwork, securing circuits of distribution, working out the costs of printing, and promoting the book for domestic and international markets. Without this type of collaboration between the writer and the editor or the publisher, which lies "outside" of narrative representation, the very existence of a text like Hagedorn's novella could not have been ensured.

Important as it is to keep in mind the exploitative structures attending globalization, a refusal to recognize the important role of the people involved in the publication of works by minorities at such an early stage in the development of multiculturalism is to take for granted the extraordinary fact that there were people who, for the first time in U.S. cultural history, were able to forcefully break down and reach across preexisting boundaries of ethnicity, race, and gender on the basis of aesthetics. Such breaking down of boundaries should not be reduced or dismissed as a mere symptom that occurs in the process of labor redistribution attending the shift into a global economic structure of the neoliberal state. On the contrary, the establishment of small literary presses was a refusal to acquiesce to that economic shift, a rare alternative to the increasing commercialization of literary works under large publishing houses that were starting to be dictated by the corporate interests of the large media conglomerates to which they were starting to contribute.

Precisely for this reason, this chapter includes a discussion of archival material in the Jessica Tarahata Hagedorn Papers and the Momo's Press

Papers at UC Berkeley, read as text with a narrative of its own. I discuss the role of people who rarely if ever appear in accounts of Hagedorn's early career, such as Hagedorn's publisher Stephen Vincent, whose presence is seemingly nowhere to be found in the novella but everywhere in the archive. Correspondences between Hagedorn and Vincent, as well as several drafts of revisions, suggest the undeniable extent to which Vincent offered his own creative vision as a part of her work, particularly in the novella "Pet Food." The archive, unlike her narrative, offers an alternative to the linear trajectory leading toward the realities of contemporary globalization and Hagedorn's own later dismissal of this earlier multicultural moment; it moves back into the past, shaping our interpretive future through excavation and reconstruction of the material past, placing value on the act of redeeming rather than discarding. Instead of simply offering standard observations and criticisms of globalization, this chapter gestures toward new possibilities opened up by globalization. If "multiculturalism" feels like an overused term in our current reality several decades later, this is a testament to the permanence with which these boundary crossings fundamentally changed the cultural imagination in the United States, bringing new voices into being.

San Francisco's Multicultural Avant-Garde Literary Scene

A snapshot of Hagedorn appears in the fifth volume of Ishmael Reed's literary journal *Yardbird Reader*, initially conceived in 1972 as "America's only annual multi-cultural reader." Hagedorn looks back at us from a photo collage playfully entitled *Yardbird Krewe*, alongside contemporary writers captured under the flash of Reed's camera. Among them are such writers as Toni Morrison and Leslie Marmon Silko, figures of the Black Arts movement including Lorenzo Thomas and Toni Cade Bambara, as well as the avant-garde writer Keith Abbott. This was a cosmopolitan set of writers gathered in the Bay Area from all over the United States, getting together with writers born abroad, not just from the Philippines but also from Panama, Nicaragua, and Puerto Rico.[17] The literary accomplishments of these writers were considerable. By 1972, Reed himself had published his highly acclaimed works *The Free-Lance Pallbearers* and *Yellow Back Radio Broke-Down* and was about to publish *Mumbo Jumbo*; Toni Morrison had just published *The Bluest Eye* and would publish her second novel, *Sula*; Toni Cade Bambara had edited the first anthology of black women writers in U.S. literary history, *The Black Woman*, and was putting together her short-story collection *Gorilla, My Love*. Moreover, literary collaborations beyond their own writing, significant contributions to the reshaping of

U.S. literary landscape, were to develop straight out of this group within a decade. Morrison would start to work with Toni Cade Bambara as her editor at Random House, while Bambara herself would coedit the groundbreaking anthology for female writers of color *The Bridge Called My Back*, edited with Gloria Anzaldúa and Cherríe Moraga. Following the success of her novel *Dogeaters*, Hagedorn would single-handedly edit a landmark anthology of Asian American literature, *Charlie Chan Is Dead*, which featured for the first time the voices of Asian American female writers and global writers who remained absent in earlier anthologies. Morrison, Bambara, and Hagedorn's work, as creators of an alternative literary space, attest to the rich possibilities Ishmael Reed first introduced through Yardbird Publishing.

Yardbird Publishing, which Reed created with Al Young upon his move to the West Coast from New York, was formed as a direct, explicit response to the difficulty that minority writers almost always faced in the publishing world.[18] The inaugural volume of the *Yardbird Reader* includes a description of (white) editors who were unaccommodating in their treatment of black writers, neglectful and careless in the handling of their manuscripts, or, in Reed's words used in the introduction of this first volume, "seek[ing] out to edit our manuscripts until the manuscripts see it their way."[19] Reed remarked that some of the best black writers were often dismissed because they "didn't respond like sheep when some abstract, nebulous symbol was invoked." Often, they were reduced to commodities, "mute dictaphones recording someone's, often, ludicrous political and social notions—slaves, standing on an auction block as our proportions and talents are discussed." As John K. Young observes about Reed's novel in the works at this time, *Flight to Canada*, in which the startling placement of modern technology within a Civil War context informs us that "the past of slavery and the present (and future) of 'freedom' inform each other at every turn, in a kind of double-sided palimpsest," Yardbird Publishing and its *Yardbird Reader* also offered a perspective on the future that was grounded in the inescapable, if culturally repressed, realities of the past.[20] Reed and others sought to challenge the continual shaping of cultural memory by a repression grounded in the past of slavery, following the lead of "the international Afro-American genius" of Charlie "Yardbird" Parker's music, which they referenced in the title of the journal, "its sound and its brilliant prismatic light, flying into the 21st century": "Our Motto: 'Once a work of art has crossed the border there are few chances of getting it back.'"

The inclusion of Jessica Hagedorn and other Asian American writers into their fold ("Krewe") is indicative of Yardbird Publishing's distinctive move away from the mono-ethnicity model that had defined black cultural nationalism of the 1960s. As is clear from the introduction in the first volume, Reed and Al Robles envisioned a radically new platform for many brilliant but marginalized artists to be in lively conversation with each other, seeking to retrieve what was lost in the prevailing attitudes of the nonwhite Establishment composed of "self-appointed guardians, interpreters and purveyors of what is officially held to be Black Culture" with "a vested interest in promoting a particular, monolithic brand of Afro-American cultures and attitudes." Reed's coeditor, Al Young, likened this to the Left in the 1930s dictating "'correct' forms of cultural expression for the revolutionary edification of the masses" in his own introduction to the first volume of *Yardbird Reader*: "Josef Stalin—who never set foot in the United States—could casually denounce jazz as a decadent bourgeois music and send countless American radical intellectuals home in a rush to revise their views on this most vital and creative of native cultural forms." Young's criticism was thus aimed at the pandering of publications like the *Black World* to "black bourgeoisie and petit-bourgeoisie," but at the same time, he was also dismissive of black street literature at a time when the underground best-selling author Iceberg Slim's *Pimp: The Story of My Life* (1967) had already sold more than 2 million copies by 1973. A new pulp industry in Los Angeles was well under way to reproduce this success, hiring writers to produce pulp fiction featuring "pimps, junkies, con men, petty thugs, extortionists, and psychopaths," which Young characterized as "Black people portraying Black people as stereotypes."

Reed's acute awareness about the difficulty that Asian American writers faced in the publishing world is perhaps most apparent in an interview he gave in 1975, in which he commented that "[big publishing companies] wouldn't publish Asian-Americans because they feel that Asians are inscrutable and are going to move to New York and move them into the Atlantic [Ocean], that's the 'Yellow Peril. . . . The reviewers out here don't like Asians except the *Pacific Sun* and the *Berkeley Gazette*."[21] While the first volume of the *Yardbird Reader* had not contained any Asian American writers, Reed invited Frank Chin and Shawn Wong to edit an Asian American issue as its third volume. This was the first Asian American anthology in literary history, actually predating the foundational 1974 anthology *AIIIEEEEE!: An Anthology of Asian American Writers* from Howard University Press, which Chin and Wong worked on with Jeffrey Paul Chan and Lawson Inada.[22] Chan and Inada had been contributors in that third issue of *Yardbird Reader*, which also included Asian American literary works by Mei(-Mei) Berssenbrugge, Al Robles, Alan

C. Lau, Hisaye Yamamoto, Wakako Yamauchi, alongside works by black poets like Stanley Eldridge and Joe Johnson, Native American writers like Ron Welburn, Leslie Marmon Silko, and Simon Ortiz, as well as the Puerto Rican poet Victor Hernandez Cruz.[23] Through another publishing house, Reed, Cannon & Johnson Communications Co., Reed would continue to publish, promote, and disseminate Asian American literary works like Cyn Zarco's poems in *Jambalaya: Four Poets*, Berssenbrugge's *Random Possession*, (Shawn) Wong's *Home Base*, and Yuri Kageyama's *Peeling*.[24]

Meanwhile, in other places in the Bay Area, pioneering attempts to provide a radically new multicultural platform were also emerging along gendered lines. Hagedorn's *Dangerous Music* was indeed promoted by Ishmael Reed, whose endorsement emphasizes Hagedorn's worldliness as well as her embeddedness in the San Francisco poetry scene: "Jessica Hagedorn is a S.F. Mambo and this *Dangerous Music* is her spirit book. The poetry and prose are worldly like much traveled baggage you bought at Lord & Taylors with inspirational stickers of all the right stops from the Philippines to New York. She is one of the queens of the marvelous San Francisco 'Ditty-Bop' school of poetry. *Dangerous Music* is a Botanical Garden."[25] Reed also ran a powerful review of *Dangerous Music* by Thulani (Nkabinde) Davis in the fifth volume of *Yardbird Reader*.[26] Yet the volume was also endorsed by the poet Alta, whose description recognizes the importance of gender at the center of her work, placing an emphasis on the politics of women's ("our") lives. Alta sees readers beginning to "recognize the voice of another human" as "[Hagedorn's] humor sets sex in a bearable light" and "her anger sees the politics of all our lives."[27]

Alta's publishing house in Oakland, Shameless Hussy Press (1969–89), is known as the first female-owned press in the United States and one of the earliest attempts to re(dis)cover texts by women writers issuing out-of-print novels like the nineteenth-century cross-dressing writer George Sand's *Lavinia* and *The Haunted Pool*, and producing an anthology of recovered texts in *Tenth Muse: Women Poets before 1806: A Rediscovery of 540 Women Poets Lost to History* (1980). Alta's aim for Shameless Hussy Press was to "piece together forgotten or silenced articulations of female experiences" that would create a "warm quilt for women," and would be very open to new narratives and literary experimentations of form by women writers.[28] It was Shameless Hussy Press that introduced works by Asian American women writers like Mitsuye Yamada's *Camp Notes and Other Poems* (1976) and Barbara Noda's *Strawberries* (1979); it was here, too, that Ntozake Shange first found a publisher for her much-celebrated choreopoem *For Colored Girls Who Have Considered Suicide, When the Rainbow Is Enuf* (1975). Other published titles from Shameless Hussy Press included revisionist accounts of history and feminist social/cultural critique, such as *Calamity Jane's Letters to Her Daughter, Herstory of Prostitution in Western Europe, Fight for Freedom: A Slave Girl's Escape, Home Front: Women and Vietnam,* and *New Plays by Women.* The name of Hagedorn's Filipino American protagonist in "Pet Food," incidentally, is George Sand, whose namesake was the very author Alta brought back into print and made once again available for contemporary readership.

Alta's multicultural vision for Shameless Hussy Press was rare among literary platforms for women writers in San Francisco at the time. Gloria E. Anzaldúa, for instance, has talked about the way that voices of Chicana poets were easily drowned out in the Feminist Writers' Guild, which was made up of almost all white and increasingly conservative middle-class members.[29] Alta's vision was not always accepted. The antagonism that Shameless Hussy Press invited from some women was in fact such that Alta felt threatened enough to move her press to San Lorenzo: "When I said I received death threats, I'm not kidding.[P]eople threatened to destroy my press, my physical AB Dick 360 offset press. I had to move to the suburbs and get a post office box and an unlisted number." Diana Press, one of the earliest feminist/lesbian presses that Shameless Hussy Press helped in setting up, was vandalized and had to close its operations in 1975.[30] According to Alta, "evidence came out . . . that it was all women who destroyed Diana Press."[31]

Third World Communications Collective was a new literary forum formed exclusively among women writers of color under these circumstances. It originally developed out of the Poncho Che Collective, a San Francisco East Bay group of cultural and political activists who had far-reaching impact on the Latino literary movement, and was run by nonwhite women writers like Nina Serrano, Ntozake Shange, Janice Mirikitani, and Geraldine Kudaka, among others. Hagedorn was a part of this different kind of multicultural forum, and worked as an editor at the Third World Communications to compile *Third World Women* (1972),[32] which was actually the first collection of literary works in U.S. cultural history by women writers of color, almost a full decade earlier than the more widely circulated and well-recognized anthologies like Anzaldúa and Moraga's *This Bridge Called My Back: Writings by Radical Women of Color* (1981) and Barbara Smith's *Home Girls* (1983) from Kitchen Table Press. Like Anzaldúa, who would go on to describe *This Bridge Called My Back* as "sweeping back against this kind of 'All of us are women and so you are included and we were all equal,'"[33] the preface of Third World Communications' *Third World Women* expressed a strong resolve among women writers of color to carve out a literary space which they could call their own:

> We have been subjugated to the Peace Corps missionary trip of white women saving us from ourselves, subjugated to racism from white women in the name of sisterhood. We have been told by white women how to relate to our men, how to raise our children. Is this not the same as the slavemaster's wife dictating to her maid how she should live?

Hagedorn's own embrace of Third World Collective, however, does not revolve around antagonism against white women writers, nor was it prompted by any immediate self-identification with the Third World. ("Were we really a part of the Third World? *The Third World.*")[34] Rather, the collective notion of "we" is most clearly defined against the norms and conventions of the mainstream publishing industry that excluded these writers: "We no longer wanted to sit around waiting for the publishing industry to notice us; we raised money, edited, designed, and published our own books, knowing all along that there was a growing readership out there."[35]

Hagedorn did express her self-identification with the writerly sensibility of postcolonial writers from Latin America who had influenced her development as a poet: "Marquez, Puig, and other Latin American writers were a revelation to me even in translation; this literature expressed a contemporary sensibility much closer to the surreal 'hothouse' sensibility of the Philippines than other Asian literatures."[36] She also shared an awareness about the English language as a historical tool of colonization, a particularly important concern among postcolonial writers, although her stance was different from Ngugi Wa Thiong'o's during the 1980s, when he famously rejected writing in English and decided to write exclusively in the native Kenyan language, Gikuyu.[37] On the contrary, among various drafts in the Jessica Hagedorn Papers, we find a passage from Salman Rushdie's *Imaginary Homelands* that expresses the notion that for some postcolonial writers, the embrace of the English language is itself important:

> I don't think it's always necessary to take up the anti-colonial—or is it post-colonial?—cudgels against English. What seems to me to be happening is that those peoples who were once colonized by the language are now rapidly remaking it, domesticating it, becoming

> more and more relaxed about the way they use it—assisted by the English language's flexibility and size, they are carving out large territories for themselves within frontiers.[38]

Here, the idea is not so much that of transforming the tool of oppression as a weapon of subversion, as Paule Marshall wrote about immigrant women of her mother's generation or as critics like Tejumola Olanyan have noted about Derek Wolcott's writing.[39] To stake out a new territory "within a closed frontier" is to imagine a way of posing a fundamental challenge to the cultural logic of imperialism that requires *actual space* in its articulation. To claim new spatiality through language and representation is to contest the very principles of the cultural imaginary at the core of imperialist fantasy. Hagedorn indicates that there is an exclusive space that can be accessed only through an acquisition of language other than English, an advancement of frontier or an expansion of territory opened up by another language: "the language(s) we speak are not necessarily the language(s) in which we dream."

This particular stance formed at the crossroads of politics and poetics leads up to a brilliant moment of tricksterism in Hagedorn's literary career, when she used the dazzling success of her National Book Award–winning novel *Dogeaters* as leverage to publish an anthology of contemporary Asian American writing from Penguin.[40] What she sought in editing the volume is apparent in a letter that she wrote inviting Maxine Hong Kingston to make a submission:

> I am definitely interested in writing that is risky, playful, and passionate—and in stories that push at the limits of language, culture, and identity. . . . I am very excited about the possibilities of this anthology and the opportunity to showcase some of the best, diverse, and most promising writers working in the English language today.[41]

The resulting volume, *Charlie Chan Is Dead*, was effectively the first anthology to introduce works by many Asian American writers to a "mainstream" audience, challenging the long-standing connection implicitly made between whiteness and aesthetic value through the very circuit of distribution that had hitherto perpetuated it. In the anthology's introduction, Hagedorn described "the long-cherished concepts of a xenophobic literary canon dominated by white heterosexual males," arguing that, "obviously, there was room for more than one voice and one vision in this ever-expanding arena." Han Ong's letter to Hagedorn about the anthology may more fully convey the radical affect at the core of the anthology: "You're right, I think, when you suggested the Penguin insignia on the cover of Charlie should have been placed in between the two pistols. Kill that motherfucking Penguin! Down with the dodo gatekeepers of the (lily white, hetero male) lit standard."[42]

A Star Is Born: Narrative Construction of the Cosmopolitan Subject in Jessica Hagedorn's "Pet Food"

In a 1974 article in a local newspaper, Jessica Hagedorn casts her work in terms that resonate with the political radicalism of the historical avant-garde, as she discusses "an urgent pressure to construct something, a collective of filmmakers, writers, musicians and technicians, a different kind of voice to counteract what media is doing to this country."[43] One way of perceiving her early work as a conscious pushback against mass media's increasing stronghold on the collective national consciousness is to consider the emphasis she placed on the performative aspect of creative expression.[44] As Christine Balance points out, "it was mainly through the event of the poetry reading—as with the political rally—that minority artists expressed a sense of urgency and need for unmediated presence through live proclamations and performance."[45] Hagedorn's stage performances in poetry readings and rock music were both grounded in the artist's actual physical presence, which could create a collective experience of a particular time and space transformed through language, which fundamentally challenges the machinery of mass media consisting of mass production, reproduction, and distribution. The ideal poetry reading would be like performing her music, "an extravaganza of voices and moving bodies playing instruments that would hypnotize an audience numbed by the pomp and circumstance of academia, forgetting that the origins of poetry are oral and physical—even Robert Bly cops to *that*."[46] The novella she was working on around the time, "Pet Food," which was performed as a musical drama before it took print form in 1981, captured a sense of the changing reality attending the structural shift into a globalized postindustrial economy including the rapid expansion of mass media, and the complex repositioning of the artist within culture industry.

In the course of telling a story about a Filipino American teenager named George Sand who aspires to become a poet and ultimately achieves some level of success as a lyricist for a Broadway musical financed by transnational capital, "Pet Food" reminds us that the trajectory of U.S. cultural history was traditionally established through a series of displacements. Toward the beginning of the narrative, Hagedorn sprinkles references to figures of Motown music and early rock and roll as we are introduced to the protagonist. The novella opens as George defiantly leaves the home she shares with her mother, planning to move to downtown San Francisco to make it on her own. Trying not to care about her mother's lack of support for this decision, George walks down the street singing "Dancing in the Street" with lyrics she makes up:

> *Little Richard /Tutti-Frutti / Fats Domino / I'm walkin' / are you ready for a brand-new beat? / Summer's here / The time is right / for dancin' in the street / Sal Mineo / James Dean / Marlon Brando / Rat-hole / Rabbit hole / and Goodbye, Feets!*[47]

The original Motown hit that George sings, a party song composed by Stevie Wonder and first recorded by Martha and the Vandellas, was a song that celebrated the notion of people brought together across the nation by the music, naming major U.S. cities: Chicago, New Orleans, New York City, Philadelphia, Baltimore, Washington, D.C., Detroit, and L.A. As Suzanne E. Smith reminds us, "Dancing in the Street" went on to become the background music for Black Detroit's 1963 march on Washington for civil rights and social justice, and thus was a strongly charged statement invoking a time of unprecedented racial and social upheaval in the United States.[48] In "Pet Food," names of these major cities are replaced by names of early rock and roll musicians from below the Mason-Dixon Line and Hollywood TV/film actors from the 1950s.

Despite the casualness with which George is supposed to have changed these lyrics, to accompany the idea of "the young rebel hero" she could hold on to, the references actually leave ample room for critical engagement. The cast of musicians named toward the beginning of the lyrics remind us of an exclusionary tradition of U.S. popular culture in which black musicians who had legitimate claims to creative expression got sidelined by white musicians, and often remained obscured and unrecognized. I will only gesture here to the excellent work by cultural historians like George Lipsitz, Richard Dyer, and Eric Lott, among others, who have shown us that "the white incorporation (or ripping off) of black music" was central to the cultural history of popular music in the United States including ragtime, the Charleston, the tango, swing, rock, and later, disco.[49] The Hollywood film industry in the 1950s seemed to offer a new venue for talented musicians like Little Richard, whose performance of "Tutti Frutti" was a feature in *Don't Knock the Rock* (1956), but this was almost immediately overshadowed by the cover of his song released that same year by Elvis Presley (who remains unnamed in George's altered lyric), as record companies started to move black singers off of the hit lists.[50]

To a certain extent, Presley's music may have challenged national and regional social conventions of race, gender, and class in Cold War America,[51] but this blatant sidelining of black musicians renders questionable how much we can say this was true, or how much he was actually responsible for reproducing that very structure. Presley's album did not credit Little Richard as the song's writer, nor did he seem to care about doing so in performances. Greil Marcus's description of Elvis Presley's performance captures this dynamic:

> "Here's a song that's real hot around the nation and some parts of Africa," Presley says to introduce the next number. "A song here recorded by a—friend of mine," he says, bending the last three words with an odd affectation, almost twirling them. The friend is Little Richard ("I never met him"), the song is "Long Tall Sally," and Elvis is instantly ripping it to shreds, rushing far out ahead of his band. Little Richard told a funny story, watching from the alley as Uncle John chased Sally out of her wig and Aunt Mary caught them; Elvis makes it clear that it's the man singing and no one else who's got his hands all over Sally, and who's not letting it go.[52]

Little Richard's "Tutti Frutti" receded into the background of U.S. popular culture as the song itself morphed into the anonymity of standard background music used in TV and Hollywood film productions over the decades to come, with the exception of John Waters's kitsch usage of the song in *Mondo Trasho* (1969). Elvis Presley's image, by contrast, saturated the cultural consciousness of his fans during those very same postwar decades, which was to remain staggeringly ubiquitous in mainstream discourse even after his death in 1977.

Besides the actors who became synonymous with the "rebel hero" they enacted, James Dean and Marlon Brando,[53] the lyrics also include the oft-forgotten gay actor Sal Mineo, who appeared alongside Dean in Norman Ray's *Rebel Without a Cause* (1955). Cultural critics like Peter Biskind pointed out in the mid-1970s that *Rebel Without a Cause* was actually a profoundly conservative film despite the appearance to the contrary,[54] and Richard Dyer agrees that it was ultimately interested in resolving the rebellion rather than promoting it. The centrality of the rebel hero, played by James Dean, often eclipses the death of the character played by Sal Mineo, although this is in fact crucial to establishing James Dean as an iconic (heterosexual) figure in the popular consciousness. Sal Mineo's character, Plato, must die in spite of his potential as a more authentic rebel, the true misfit in the social fabric bearing an ultimately irreconcilable relationship to the nuclear family scheme, exhibiting a kind of desperation lacking in the James Dean character. This narrative contradiction makes sense only if we factor in the nature of Hollywood film production as a capitalist enterprise that privileges commercial success over ideological cohesion. In Fredric Jameson's view. successful commercial films very often offer a way of opening up and airing social tensions in order to contain them.[55] Again, the star image of the "rebel hero" cannot exist without an obscuring of its dark double, not just from the film itself but from the entire iconography of postwar popular culture.

The long-standing history of cultural displacement that shaped the history of U.S. popular music was central to Alice Walker's short story "Nineteen Fifty-Five" (1971), about a black female singer named Gracie Mae Still, also called "Little Mama," who signs away her song and the remainder of her unsold records to the agent of a young Elvis Presley–like singer later dubbed the "Emperor of Rock and Roll." While the singer, Traynor, admits to not fully understanding the meaning of Gracie Mae's song, he is still able to produce a perfect imitation of Gracie Mae's performance, "following every turning of [her] voice, side streets, avenues, red lights, train crossings and all," driving "little white girls wild" with a "nasty little jerk he was doing from the waist down,"[56] as Elvis had done in 1956 with Willa Mae "Big Mama" Thornton's "Hound Dog."[57] Traynor goes on to make millions off of Gracie Mae's song, although Walker chooses to highlight the status of the song as one that has been cancelled out or is to be filled in, by calling the song "————." In Walker's story, Traynor suffers a lifetime of mostly repressed guilt, and from time to time tries to make amends by sending gifts to Gracie Mae, finally arriving at a gesture of recognition and appreciation when he arranges to have her perform "her song" on the *Johnny Carson Show.* The point being made by the subsequent reaction of his impressively unimpressed fans is that it is in the interstitial spaces of Walker's short story, in the realm outside the machinery of mass culture industry, where Gracie Mae can be restored to full personhood, undefeated, warm, sensible, and the ever-sassy (-in-old-age) blues singer whose general happiness suggests that no amount of "greatness" achieved through the sale of stolen goods can bring that which can never be bought.

In Hagedorn's novella, Little Richard gets sidelined once more as George thinks back longingly about going to see Jimi Hendrix at the Pop Festival of 1967: "Who was this outrageous black man with the dangerous hair and those two foreign-looking white boys in the background as his *sidemen???* . . . He wasn't even Little Richard. Everyone could dismiss him as some legendary rock'n'roll faggot. He was Jimi Hendrix—sticking his pretty pink tongue out at all the women in the audience, maybe even the men" (111). Hendrix reversed the dynamic on "cultural thievery" by doing very successful covers of Elvis Presley songs, but what is most important here is that he does so as a global figure. Hendrix registers in George's consciousness as a guitar player leading a new band from the United Kingdom, rather than as a musician from Seattle or New York. This global register offers a critical distance to discussions of race and U.S. popular culture bounded within U.S. domestic history. If we are to be wary of what Leerom Medovoi called a "producer-based model of autonomous artistic development," and take a moment to truly think about the consumerist dimension of a song like Little Richard's "Good Golly, Miss Molly," which hinges on an interesting moment of crossover identification experienced on the part of white fans,[58] we need to also think about the global consumption of that same song. Race does not operate in quite the same way when there is a transnational dimension. bell hooks is aware of this global register, for instance, when she argues that the focus on the "crossover" phenomenon (of musicians like Stevie Wonder, Michael Jackson, etc. being accepted by the white audience)[59] is a deflection from the fact that white cultural appropriations of black culture are a part of the reality that shape the lives of black people who are "daily resisting racism, advocating ongoing decolonization, and in need of effective black liberation struggle" at present.

By the time Hagedorn was devoting her energies to the drafting of "Pet Food" in the late 1970s, the market for popular music production was fully globalized, reaching beyond the confines of the nation. "Dancing in the Street," which was first recorded in 1964, saw a revival in 1969 with the Vandellas' success in the United Kingdom. As Arjun Appadurai would note in *Modernity at Large*, the uncanny Filipino affinity for U.S. popular culture can be seen as a "rich testimony to the ever-expanding global culture of the hyperreal ("An entire nation seems to have learned how to mimic Kenny Rogers and Lennon Sisters, like a vast Asian Motown chorus").[60] Hagedorn's own account of U.S. popular culture during the 1950s and 1960s in the Philippines shows this to also be the social reality particular to a colonized nation. "It was pretty clear to most of us," Hagedorn wrote in the introduction to *Charlie Chan Is Dead*, "that what was important, what was inevitably preferred, was the aping of our mythologized Hollywood universe. The colonization of our imagination was relentless and hard to shake off. Everywhere we turned, the images held up did not match our own. In order to be acknowledged, we had to strive to be as American as possible."[61] To the global audience, American cities (in the original "Dancing in the Street" lyrics, for example) are mostly an idealization, no longer anchored in historicity or actual geographic locations populated with real people. Seeping beyond the American imaginary with the increasing global circulation of the "hyperreal," they become a set of cultural symbols that creates and feeds lack and desire shaping lives worldwide.

"Pet Food" anticipates the multiple cultural displacements that the song "Dancing in the Street" would endure shortly after its own publication. Soon after the commercial success of Van Halen's 1982 version of the song distributed by Warner Brothers, U.K. musicians David Bowie and Mick Jagger's 1984 version of "Dancing in the Street" made changes that seemingly factored in the global in its altered lyrics. "OK, talk to you," Bowie says in his preamble to the song, in a gesture that seemingly embraces a wider global audience: "South America, Australia, France, Germany, UK, Africa." The altered lyrics in their version of "Dancing in the Street" tries to imagine a global populism that can reach across the Cold War structure, now adding "the streets of Brazil / Back in the USSR" and "Cross in China too." Typical of a widely shared but skewed worldview, however, Bowie and Jagger's lyrics treat the entire continent of Africa as though it were a single country like Australia, France, Germany, the United Kingdom, China, and the USSR. *Non*-communist nations in Asia are completely absent from the worldview, when it is surely imperative for any legitimate claim to populism on a global scale at this time to recognize the existence of the rapidly industrializing nations in Southeast Asia,[62] with a vast number of its workers co-opted to shoulder the burden of industrial production based on cheap labor and inadequately protected workers' rights, which effectively sustain the emerging postindustrial economy of the "Free World."

Hagedorn's own references in "Dancing in the Street" gesture toward an imperialist origin and nature of the globalized postindustrial economy, by referencing Lewis Carroll's *Alice's Adventures in Wonderland* ("*Goodbye Feets!*"), which links George's startup in an appropriately bohemian setting of a dingy artist apartment ("rat-hole") to the rabbit hole that leads Alice to Wonderland. The phrase "*Goodbye Feets!*" appears in the section of *Wonderland* when Alice magically grows so tall that she can no longer see her feet. Becoming emotional over the fact that her feet would now be left to fend for themselves, Alice will then cry a "Pool of Tears" that she will need to swim through. Yet there is a flicker of some shrewd mental calculation in her otherwise sentimental and sympathetic musings, as she considers the fact that she must secure control over her feet even if she stopped taking proper care of them:

> "Oh, my poor little feet, I wonder who will put on your shoes and stockings for you now, dears? I'm sure *I* shan't be able! I shall be a great deal too far off to trouble myself about you: you must manage the best way you can;—but I must be kind to them," thought Alice, "or perhaps they won't walk the way I want to go! Let me see: I'll give them a new pair of boots every Christmas."

If Alice is to be properly read as a "child imperialist" as Daniel Bivons has argued,[63] one should also consider the many disenfranchised lives of the colonized, saddled with the weight of the British Empire. In order to secure the stability and comfort of life for British subjects, complete with (in all probability) smiling children getting Christmas presents every year, countless lives toil beyond their direct purview, under various modes of colonial exploitation, from trans-Atlantic triangular trade to slave and coolie labor. Any disturbing unsightliness is kept across the ocean so that most imperial subjects never have to think about them except when inconvenienced or feeling charitable. The legacies of Western imperialisms will continue to shape the world, taking on a different form under globalization, as offshore and service labor that stabilizes the reality of Michael Hardt and Antonio Negri's model of "Empire."

This idea of Hagedorn's protagonist as a modern-day Alice also suggests that she is a close approximation of her namesake, George Sand, resituated in the United States at the end of the twentieth century and recontextualized by the structures of late capitalism. The narrative trajectory of the novella recalls to mind the biographical trajectory of the legendary nineteenth-century French author who broke away from her leisurely status to pursue a new undertaking and identity as a writer. In 1821, George Sand wrote the following sentence in a letter to her mother, often seen as a self-defining moment in her career as a writer: "j'ai dix-sept ans et je sais marcher" (I am seventeen years old and know how to walk [on my own]).[64] Needless to say, George Sand's Paris in the nineteenth century was also the heart of the autocratic regime of the Second Empire, which conducted an aggressive foreign policy based on continuing expansion of its colonies (Senegal and Indochina) and its subsequent importing of low-wage African and Asian workers from former colonies. The prolific production of Sand's novels actually coincides with the fall of the Second Republic and the inauguration of the Second Empire. Hagedorn's Filipino American George Sand can thus serve as a critique of cultural fetishism surrounding the original George Sand. Read as a vicious satire, Hagedorn's novella has the effect of urging readers to look beyond the mythical figure of the artist, safely protected under the wings of Empire, and to perceive the more difficult realities of imperialism at hand in both the past and the present. The stylistic fragmentation prominent in Hagedorn's novella, often seen as a stock characteristic of literary postmodernism, can also be read more cogently as an embittered response to the restructuring of U.S. imperialism in the light of multinational capitalism and new forms of domination.[65]

On one level, Hagedorn's novella participates in restoring the historical significance of George Sand, the nineteenth-century writer, a much-needed feminist intervention at the time of its publication when Sand's novels had long gone out of print in the United States. In *Braided Lives* (1982), a novel by Hagedorn's contemporary Marge Piercy set in 1950s Detroit, George Sand's name appears as a reference made by another young female protagonist aspiring to be a poet. George Sand appears in the short list of women she admires, though the protagonist admits the lack of access to her work: "I can't find any of her books in the library but I read about her in a biography of Chopin."[66] In Piercy's novel, cross-dressing appears as more of a fleeting trope, such as when the protagonist runs out from home to venture out into the streets, and we are told that in jeans and jacket and her brother's cap she can pass for a boy: "I know that too is somehow wicked but it gives me a free pass through these blocks" (30). In Hagedorn's novella, in which the protagonist takes on George Sand's name, there is more at work than a simple recovery of this figure. The reference to Sand is an embodiment that introduces readers to the more subtle and ambivalent relationship of Sand's literary work to the oppressive structure of imperialism, remapped now, within the structure of globalization.

George Sand, née Amandine Aurore Lucie Dupin (1804–1876), is often overshadowed by literary giants such as Flaubert, Stendhal, and Balzac, who are often seen as the three major writers who established the primacy of the French novel in the nineteenth century. Sand's pastoral novels have tended to be cast aside and even derided at times.[67] This is to be expected, as Sand's recuperation of rural life in her pastoral novels serves as a countercultural critique of modernity itself.[68] Her positioning within Western modernity can be read from her inclination to write a counternarrative, rather than a reproduction, of the Faust legend. In *The Seven Strings of Lyre* (1838), for instance, Sand responded to Goethe's *Faust* in a philosophical play by taking Helen of Troy (Hélène) as a focal point. Instead of being cast in the role of the devastatingly beautiful femme fatale conjured up from hell to awaken Faust's passions and secure his damnation, Helen of Troy is described as "a symbol of the beauty and naturalness of classical antiquity";[69] she is in fact the protector of the magic lyre that Mephistopheles must destroy in order to win the soul of Master Albertus, who is a descendant of Faust and his mistress Marguerite. Despite Mephistopheles's concerted ploys to debase Helen in Albertus's eyes or to incite his lust, Albertus's constant love for the "daughter of poetry" becomes the "seventh string" that saves him from his fate even when he breaks all six strings of the lyre: "from now on, his soul will be a lyre whose strings will all resound to faith, and whose canticle will mount toward God on the wings of hope and joy" (178). Sand complicates the Faustian model by the sublimation of the femme fatale, which illuminates the problems in the structure of modernity that requires a depiction of the female body as an evil and inhuman entity, often marginalized and used as foil to establish the centrality and morality of the (male) modern protagonist.

What is most appropriate about the parallel between the two Georges is that although the original George Sand's humanitarian concerns helped raise important questions about the living conditions of (urban working-class) women in France, her concerns did not reach out toward the living conditions of women in French colonies; despite her considerable knowledge, Sand's frequent references to slavery were "always expressed in guarded, often cryptic ways."[70] Similarly, Hagedorn's George Sand stops short of grappling with the reality of the structure of Empire and the role of the United States at the end of the twentieth century. In the novella, George agrees to write a Broadway musical about "the nightmares of American life" from the point of view of a Filipino American subject, but what she produces does not actually bridge the gap that exists between herself and the exploited bodies of the Third World. Only at the very end of the novella, when she decides to leave both the musical project and the framework of the novella altogether, does she become emotionally aware of her own bodiliness, experiencing aches and the "sudden rushes" of the body. George disappears into the night at the end of the novella: "My bones ached, and I felt a sudden rush as I walked down the street. It was always that way with me when it was time for me to go" (145).

The Death of the Artist: Narrative Construction of the Cosmopolitan Subject in Jessica Hagedorn's "Pet Food," Side B

The musical drama version of "Pet Food," written in 1979, starts with the following voice-over in the stage script, indicating that there is another character who is just as important to "Pet Food" as George herself: "I just want to tell you a story. How I finally came to be who I am, how I sank so low and then pulled myself back up—enduring it—and how my friend Boogie—my dear fragile friend Leopoldo Makaliwanag—lived and died." These were in fact the closing sentences in the first draft of "Pet Food," submitted to her editor, Stephen Vincent, in 1981. Indeed, George's story cannot be told without the presence of this character, Boogie, a pianist friend she made in high school and a collaborator for the Broadway production. Boogie's significance is underscored toward the beginning of the novella, when Silver Daddy, a character most often read as Kenneth Rexroth, says that "*the* George Sand" was "a most interesting personality—particularly when she ran around with that musician, Chopin!" (99). While the dialogic trajectory of the protagonist is often perceived as central, displacements needed to establish that centrality is just as "central" to the narrative. Alex Woloch illuminates this brilliantly in *One Vs. the Many* when he upholds a dialectical model as an organizing principle of the traditional novel, in which "the protagonist, whose identity rests on a narrative centrality that always threatens to take the form of wrath (erasing or absorbing all the other persons who surround him), and the minor characters who, simply through their subordinated multiplicity hover vulnerably on the borderline between name and number."[71]

Boogie's real name is Leopoldo Makaliwanag, and he is described as a Filipino American coming from a "hardworking, lower-middle-class family that always found it difficult to make ends meet." He is also referred to as "the Boogie Man" (129), which is appropriate for his increasingly haunting presence in the text, and with the fact that he is associated with a Third World presence in the United States that George is able to escape. If George is able to perform a godlike transcendence as a narrator, Boogie, like his name, is caught up in a kind of "dance," bound to corporeality and limited in the range of its movement.[72] There seems to be no striking differences in their physical appearances, and George herself often stresses their likeness in appearance and dismisses differences in subject position and power. "We were two wayward Filipino kids in torn jeans and tattered velvet shirts" (106), we are told, and she is seen posing questions like, "what's the difference between him and us?" (131). In a deleted section of the first draft of "Pet Food," she refers to both of them as "brown faces like pumas in the jungle."

At the same time, George does meticulously record her mother's adamant insistence on their differences, in which Boogie is particularized as "an American-born Pinoy with no class" (80), at various times described as the "smelly friend of yours," a "low-life fairy," "no good—a drug addict with too many crazy ideas" who is "going to drag you down with him" (81), and "nothing but a lazy drug addict fronting himself off as a piano player" (125). She almost succeeds in convincing the reader of the authenticity of this representation, an impression that "George and her family, because they are upper class, seem to be less foreign, less immigrant, than Boogie's family."[73] Moments when George romanticizes Boogie's class identity, such as when she comments that "he has always been very pretty. . . . His eclectic way of dressing never betrayed the toughness behind the elegance, and I loved the way his beauty drove men and women crazy" (99), says less about Boogie himself than it does about a sense of lack produced by the very denial of her own excess.

The global migration of Boogie's family is one fraught with the kind of difficulty remarkably absent from George's own transnationalism. The novella indicates George's privileged background through an anecdote about her American father in the Philippines, who had once declined an invitation from the president of the Philippines ("my dear, I've been invited by a better class of people, in my time"). By contrast, Boogie talks about the hard life his parents endured as immigrants: "all I have to do is listen to my father talk in his broken English. . . . Look at his worn-out hands. See my mother's shy and frightened face whenever she gets on a bus. They're permanent immigrants in this lousy place, and I've stopped asking myself why they even bothered coming here" (102). Aihwa Ong's work on the forms of global citizenship in *Neoliberalism as Exception* is particularly useful in explaining this relationship between George and Boogie. As she writes: "In global circuits, educated and self-propulsive individuals claim citizenship-like entitlements and benefits, [even] at the expense of territorialized citizens. Expatriate talents constitute a form of movable entitlement without formal citizenship. Low-skill citizens and migrants . . . are constructed as excludable populations in transit, shuttled in and out of zones of growth. People with cultural capital like George, can claim 'a form of movable entitlement' at the expense of someone like Boogie, who is among the 'territorialized citizens.'"

In fact, George's political unconscious finds its most striking expression in a nightmare she has, in which she imagines herself to be back in the Philippines, under attack by a guerrilla. Symbolizing the repressed feminized *Other* in George's psyche, Boogie returns in this dream as her assassin:

> "The killer is a beautiful young man. He looks like you, Boogie. High cheekbones, smooth copper-colored skin, straight blue-black hair. His lovely eyes pierce the darkness in my bed as he finds me, cowering. He bends his sullen face toward mine. I am gazing into his glistening eyes, thinking of my father sleeping in the third

> bedroom. I am sure the young man is going to kiss me, but he slits my throat instead. Quietly and efficiently. I've been spared hearing my father die—." (104)

Though both Boogie and George might be described as having "high cheekbones, smooth copper-colored skin, straight blue-black hair," this is a moment when George completely disavows her own likeness to the killer. Suddenly taking on the role of the little girl to be protected at all times, she casts Boogie as the threatening exoticized body, while in reality, he bears as little relationship to the Filipino terrorist as George herself. George doesn't seem to register the contradiction in the fact that unlike herself, who grew up in the Philippines when she was very young, Boogie was born in the United States and has "never even seen" the islands.

By racializing Boogie here and elsewhere, turning him into a terrorizing figure, George succeeds in setting herself apart from a Third World presence through her narrative, defining herself against Boogie as a privileged global subject. George's fantasy, told to Boogie in a gesture of intimacy, is in fact an enactment of "murder" that confines Boogie to otherness or as a "tropical apparition." So we might actually say that it is George who is guilty of "quietly and efficiently" betraying Boogie, all the while insisting on her friendship for him, and it is Boogie who must experience the feeling that "the young man (George) is going to kiss me, but he slits my throat instead." Insofar as the protagonist cannot exist without the offsetting death of a minor character, this is true, which becomes a metaphor for the way in which the notion of the cosmopolitan global subject cannot exist without the exilic and disavowed global migrant, and becomes complicit in perpetuating a structure that renders underprivileged global migrants voiceless. It is Boogie who is ultimately Hagedorn's tragic hero, standing in to represent notions of revolution, populism, and art depicted as being absent from commodified popular culture. The description of George in the opening scene invoking an American soldier dispatched to Vietnam ("like a son being sent off to an unpopular war") comes full circle here with the casting of Boogie as the Vietcong guerrilla killer ("the killer looks like you").

Accordingly, in the novella, George becomes an actual (albeit unwitting) accomplice to Boogie's actual murder, as he dies from her "birthday present," "a mighty fix" delivered by George's patron/gangster lover/drug supplier, Doctor T (143). When George writes a poem for Boogie's birthday, she casts Boogie as a "dying" animal who sheds light on the underworld, singing a "corrupt song," so that her own closeness to Boogie as a collaborator in the Broadway musical is erased:

dying fawn
sun of anubis
yr corrupt song
is choreographed by the supremes

the white bandit
holds you by the neck
on a diamond-studded leash
or is it the silver conch belt
of jimi's corpse? (137)

The "supremes" that choreograph Boogie's musical talents are embodied by two characters who jointly invest in the production of the Broadway play, Dr. T and Prince Genji. Of the two, it is Prince Genji who commissions the music for a Broadway play that has "never been done before" and is about "people like us," eventually convincing Boogie that he is fundamentally indebted to him and making Boogie consent to the exploitation of his labor: "If it weren't for him, I'd be nobody" (130). Again, Boogie's enslavement (a figure who is collared and held by the neck) is a representation that allows George to disavow her own consent to a parallel relationship that she has with *her* patron and lover, Dr. T. In her role as a narrator, George also has the power to turn herself into one of the "supremes" who choreograph Boogie's "corrupt song" and take on the role of a "white bandit" rather than the "dying fawn."

Instead of receiving this poem, Boogie dies from an overdose of drugs, and cocaine consumption becomes a color-coded metaphor that ascribes a racial dimension to the master-slave relationship between a figure that possesses whiteness (Prince Genji, George) and a darker figure who is exploited (Boogie). What seems striking here is the expression "the *white* bandit," which describes "the supremes" as a racial category of whiteness that depends here on the division of labor and not on physical attributes. George's whiteness is attained through her writing that allows her to represent herself as white; Prince Genji's whiteness is a relative notion that emerges in and through the exploitation of Boogie's labor. George, Prince Genji, and Boogie all have Asian bodies that operate on slightly different subject positions: a half-Filipino and half-American global subject born in the Philippines and brought to the United States in her childhood (George), a fully Japanese subject in the United States to enhance his economic and cultural capital (Prince Genji), and a working-class

Filipino American subject (Boogie). At the beginning of the novella, George is dangerously close to being cast in Boogie's role, as the two "beautiful young men" stare at George "like two preening leopards purring before the kill" (108), but as the narrative progresses, Boogie becomes "smaller and thinner," and his skin starts to have "a jaundiced tinge" (129). Through this triangulation, Hagedorn sketches out different ways in which the two global subjects who come from privilege are able to racialize Boogie, ironically the only actual American in the threesome.

Hagedorn grants an almost lyrical quality to the description of Boogie's death that is uncannily evocative of the demise of the eighteenth-century revolutionary Jean-Paul Marat, made famous in Jacques-Louis David's iconic painting *The Death of Marat*: "crumpled up in the shower—his face blue and serene, the remains of a mighty fix scattered on the floor around him, blood and water flowing down the drain" (143). The image of a dead poet in a bathtub, which had appeared twice in earlier points of the novella, and in Rick Powell's original illustration to "Pet Food" reinforces this feeling. A reference to Marat would underscore the idea that George's identity is socially at odds with Boogie's, just as Marat's assassin, Charlotte Corday, came from a family of poor aristocrats. The famous anecdote that Corday was able to kill him by pretending to be his friend is a famous one, and the reference suggests that in "Pet Food," George's friendship to Boogie is false, and that George is actually Boogie's killer. Insofar as the protagonist cannot exist without the offsetting death of a minor character, this is true, which becomes a metaphor for the way in which the notion of the cosmopolitan global subject cannot exist without the exilic and disavowed global migrant, of late often registering as "illegal immigrants," and becomes complicit in perpetuating a structure that renders underprivileged global migrants voiceless. Again, it is Boogie who is ultimately Hagedorn's tragic hero, standing in to represent notions of revolution, populism, and art depicted as being absent from commodified popular culture.

The different subject positions that are mapped out in the novella find a historical context in the emergence of a newly restructured form of coloniality and racialization that is shaped by an emerging multinational capitalism, crystallized by GATT and the consolidation of the Group of Seven (G7) summit meetings starting in 1975. This is a radical shift from earlier moments of colonial history in the Philippines, which were initially defined by various *competing* imperialisms at different moments, namely through occupations by Spain (1560s–1898), the United States (1898–1941), and Japan (1941–45), each vying for the increasing economic, political, military interests to be gained in their access to inexpensive raw materials, cheap labor, and expanded market for new opportunities of investments.[74] Noam Chomsky has pointed out that the United States succeeded in preventing Japan from organizing its own economic bloc in Southeast Asia that excluded the United States after World War II, but the actual securing of Southeast Asia under U.S. hegemony is accomplished by pressuring Japan to break off trade ties with China and become a Free Trade nation. The historical crystallization of post-Vietnam global structures during the Cold War decades depended on the securing of Southeast Asia under U.S. hegemony via the incorporation of Japan in the formerly competing imperialist free trade nations, consolidated as Empire. As this global formation starts to visibly take shape in the 1970s, it casts a new shadow on underprivileged Second and Third World nations as they jointly become a steady source of "internal consolidation of power and privilege."[75]

If George's name invokes the image of Western modernity through associations with her nineteenth-century namesake, Prince Genji's name is also strongly associated with the image of Empire. In fact, George and Prince Genji might be described as two sides of the same coin, and Prince Genji explicitly claims to be another version of George. "We are quite alike, you and I," he says to George, "you don't understand me, because you refuse to face your nightmares" (113). An incarnation of a literary character from Japanese literature, Prince Genji is the main protagonist of Lady Murasaki's *The Tale of Genji*, one of the first novelistic representations from Japan's Heian period (795–1185), which narrates the exiled life of an illegitimate prince through his romantic tales of female conquest/patronage. Though the imperialism of the Heian period did not depend on colonization beyond the Sea of Japan, this figure serves to effectively invoke Japan's long history of feudalism and the construction of its national identity as an empire. In the novella, Prince Genji represents the emptying out of the political significance of Japanese Empire after World War II: "How do you think I feel, being the bastard son of an emperor who is no longer fashionable? . . . My mother was a hostess at the Queen Bee Cabaret in Tokyo. My supposedly invincible father surrendered his country. My mother was paid off. I was sent to Europe to learn the Western ways of life—Paris, Florence, London, and even Budapest" (112). Japanese assimilation into the Western paradigm of modernization historically starts in the nineteenth century, but here, Hagedorn's images correctly invokes the extent to which Western modernity creates a lack in an otherwise privileged contemporary male Japanese figure that drives him to redefine his Self by turning a Third World figure into an *Other*.

As two figures of privilege emerging from older forms of imperialisms, now reinscribing themselves in the structures of global hegemony, Prince Genji and George Sand are "quite alike," Prince Genji being the figure that clarifies George Sand's unacknowledged role within the globalized world. Prince Genji describes the musical production that enslaves Boogie as merely his latest "investment": "Would you rather I invested in oil, perhaps? Or coffee beans? No one knows it, but the price of coffee is going UP. And we're going to have an oil crisis very soon. And how about commodities. Pork bellies and winter wheat. Grain futures. *Invisible things.* Don't you think I've done that all already? Pet food, for instance. Did you know that's a safe and sound investment? I'm surprised at you, George Sand . . . Because you're being so mundane this evening" (111). The culture industry, then, is characterized as simply another industry that produces new representations to appease or accommodate the lifestyle of the American consumer, pumping out new products as its "fresh meat" and "young blood" (110), or pet food; its production and its enjoyment depend on ignoring the exploited labor of Third World bodies like Boogie's that are bound, queered, and killed off. This characterization is aptly symbolized by a historicizing of Jimi Hendrix's death and the stirrings of a new Silicon Valley economy defined by speculation and investment in technology ("*invisible things*"). In the poem, the operative metaphor of Empire is seen in the description of the diminished status of Boogie; the "diamond studded leash" or "the silver conch belt of jimi's corpse" that holds Boogie by the neck can be described as the new accent of imperial leather.

By introducing a cosmopolitan subject like George as a central Asian American character, Hagedorn's novella joins, and radically alters, the tradition of feminist criticism of her contemporary moment that pointed out the negative implications of the original George Sand's own legendary cross-dressing. In *The Madwoman in the Attic* (1979), published two years prior to the publication of the novella "Pet Food," Sandra Gilbert and Susan Gubar were pointing out that the impersonation of maleness in the original George Sand's cross-dressing leaves the condition of women unchanged, still treated as "'lesser subjects' and 'lesser lives' which had constrained her foremothers."[76] This critique would also apply to the Filipino American George Sand in "Pet Food." As a protagonist of the bildungsroman who sets out to become a writer, George inherits a narrative form that traditionally centered around a male protagonist who leaves behind the domestic realm of tradition, the past, and stasis most often embodied by women. In the case of "Pet Food," George's cross-dressing perpetuates a structure that not only marginalizes women but also confines less fortunate Filipino American characters who are also male but are turned into effeminate, emasculated, or queered subjects.

One way that "Pet Food" resolves this structural problem is through ironic distance placed between Hagedorn herself and the character, George Sand, and through the portrayal of an extremely vibrant cast of marginal characters who refuse to be forgotten. One might argue that narrative violence is somewhat diminished through critical reading practice that the novella encourages. As long as the reader focuses on George, the novella feels fragmented, and the novella's marvelous coherence materializes only when we pay attention to the margins and think about what they stand for. As with all successful postcolonial writers, Hagedorn is still implicated in the postindustrial economy, but her writing proposes a different way of seeing that is not simply a "decentering" that relies on a reproduction of another center. In the now classic essay that was published four years after "Pet Food," "Three Women's Texts and a Critique of Imperialism," Gayatri Spivak showed us the flickering presence at the farthest reaches of the narrative in nineteenth-century British literature: "To pay attention to 'worlding' of what is now called 'The Third World' seems to offer one way of resolving the history of colonialism, allowing us to consider the Third World as distant cultures, exploited but with rich intact literary heritages waiting to be recovered, interpreted, and curricularized in English translation fosters the emergence of 'the Third World' as a signifier that allows us to forget that 'worlding.'"[77]

Considered in its entirety, the collection of poetry and prose *Pet Food and Tropical Apparitions* is a text that invites us to engage with that presence through her portrayals of "tropical apparitions." "Pet Food" takes up a large portion of the volume, but while it does become the centerpiece of the volume, the shorter poems offer extraordinary portrayals of "Third World" presence that offsets George's narrative trajectory in "Pet Food." In the opening poem, "Motown/ Smokey Robinson," Hagedorn speaks to a Filipino girl who came to California "in 1959 in a second-class boat / cryin' all the while cuz you didn't want to leave the barrio," linking the colonial spaces of "manila" and "the mission" with the inner city spaces of "Chinatown / east l.a. / harlem, and fillmore st." The poem extricates Smokey Robinson's song from the commodification process of the culture industry:

hey girl, you sleep without dreams
and remember the barrios and how it's all the same:
manila / the mission / Chinatown/ east l.a. / harlem /

fillmore st.
and you're gettin' kinda fat and smokey robinson's getting'
old

ooh baby baby baby
ooh baby baby
ooh

but he still looks good!!!

i love you
          i need you
          i need you
          i want you
          ooh ooh
          baby baby
          ooh (81–82)

A song that is "getting' old" may translate as a loss of market value in the culture industry, but the poet offers it as a gift to the girl who is "getting' kinda fat" and sleeps "without dreams": "*he still looks good!!!*" The poet's articulated love/need/want for this particular subject as her audience overlaps with the girl's own love of her baby, and both become images that reinfuse the fragments of the Smokey Robinson song rescued from outdatedness and obscurity. In doing so, the poet transforms this "tropical apparition" into *his* or *her* "baby," so that the process of writing is reimagined through the vantage point of the "third world mother." Taking a figure so violently brutalized by Western modernity, the poem recuperates the lost beauty of its original significance.

Stephen Vincent, Momo's Press, and the Crafting of "Pet Food"

The Jessica Hagedorn Papers at UC Berkley's Bancroft Library contain an unexpectedly small amount of written correspondence from Kenneth Rexroth. They do not belie their close relationship, but on a practical level, written evidence of his involvement with her early career, based on what one can find in Jessica Hagedorn Papers, is minimal. He reminds her, for instance, to contact a photographer who was doing a book on San Francisco poets (Christa Fleischmann), or extends an informal invitation to do a reading at UC Santa Barbara, where he lectured from 1968 to 1973. Rexroth's correspondence is easily surpassed by that of his wife, Carol Tinker, who also promoted Hagedorn's work ("If you have any clippings and PR on the group you read with, the black–Chicano–Third

World scene, send it to me & I'll try to get something going with arts and lecture") and played an important role in the publication of the Rexroth-edited anthology *Four Young Women*. It is easy to see that it was Tinker who saw through the actual process of marketing and working out the details of the anthology's publication. As she lamented in a letter addressed to Hagedorn, the prospect of this anthology had not readily come about: "the proposed anthology is still hung up—nothing from Mary yet. Trying to get things going."[78] Tinker dealt with much of the pragmatic side and the material process of publication and distribution, such as negotiating the terms of Hagedorn's contract at a complicated time when the publishers Herder-Herder and McGraw were soon to merge, making sure that the terms were fair for the contributors "since poets do not have agents to protect them,"[79] and finalizing a contract that she sent Hagedorn to sign and return on July 12, 1973.

By far the most significant amount of correspondence toward the beginning of Hagedorn's career, however, belongs to the San Francisco poet and publisher Stephen Vincent. Among the first to recognize the brilliance of Hagedorn's writing, long before the publication of her landmark novel crowned by the National Book Award, *Dogeaters*, Vincent had taken on the task of publishing the first two volumes of Hagedorn's collected poems: *Dangerous Music* (1975) and *Pet Food and Tropical Apparitions* (1981) from Momo's Press, his small literary publishing house launched in 1972. Though these two volumes may now be relatively unknown, eclipsed by the literary fame of *Dogeaters*, these publications helped her secure the interest of the literary agent who could introduce her writing to mainstream publishing houses, once she arrived in New York in 1978. Though others may have done so as well, Vincent was one person who advised her to find an agent, telling her that they can "bargain, negotiate, and protect in ways that you or I have little knowledge of."[80] The volumes are also important because they allow us to perceive Hagedorn's literary background in poetry, while observing her very first engagement with prose fiction, necessary if we want to fully appreciate the hard work that went into developing her writing to the level of *Dogeaters*.

Stephen Vincent is actually briefly introduced in Hagedorn's preface to *Danger and Beauty*, a collection of her San Francisco poems repackaged by Penguin and published along with her newer poems written in New York:

> I meet the poet Stephen Vincent at a reading I give in Berkeley around 1974. My work by then is becoming more rhythmic and

> musically influenced, meant to be "performed" before an audience. I dream about putting a band together. A dance band around words. Other poets understand the need for this. I am encouraged to dream more dreams. It is 1974 in the Bay Area and anything is possible. Stephen is interested in editing a collection for a new press, which he calls Momo's Press. The first book of poems and prose is called *Dangerous Music*, published in 1975—the same year I form my band, The West Coast Gangster Choir. I am consumed by music. How to fit rock 'n' roll into such dark words?[81]

By the time Hagedorn first met Vincent, he had already launched Momo's Press and was editing its literary journal, *Shocks*. Of her audience, only a handful of people would have been in a position to have observed the Bay Area poetry scene as closely as Vincent, whose detailed knowledge of its permutations throughout the 1960s and early 1970s is on display in his resourceful essay "Poetry Readings/Reading Poetry: San Francisco Bay Area, 1958–1980." As a graduate student at San Francisco State, Vincent had been exposed to the work of a broad range of poets who read at the Poetry Center, founded in the 1950s by Ruth Witt-Diamant and Robert Duncan. This included major San Francisco poets like Duncan himself, Kenneth Rexroth, Lew Welch, Gary Snyder, Jack Gilbert, and Helen Adam, poets from the Midwest, and John Logan, Robert Mezey, and LeRoi Jones, as well as Charles Tomlinson from the United Kingdom. Vincent himself was a poet, a part of the local poetry scene revolving around Blue Unicorn in Haight-Ashbury, a coffeehouse that was home to poets like Gene Fowler, Hilary Ayer, Ed Bullins, Jim Thurber, Doug Palmer, David Hoag, Steve Gaskin, David Sandberg, and Norm Moser. At the time, he was also the director of the NEA-funded Poetry in the Schools Program, and was in charge of placing poets of different stripes in the schools all over the Bay Area and Northern California, from surrealists, Third World writers, feminists, antiwar activists, to campus-identified poets and their creative writing students. What is often easy to forget, ironically, is that none of this was easy to do. At a time when multiculturalism was not a widely accepted practice but a challenging of the status quo, Vincent's inclusive vision accordingly sparked considerable enmity from whites who felt that it was a form of betrayal. As he recalls, "it upset the conventional, mostly white applecart, for a lot of people—which, though I took a lot of heat, was great."[82]

In a 1975 interview, Ishmael Reed refers to Momo's Press as another pioneering publishing house at the forefront of multiculturalism, very much like his own, striving to create an expansive and inclusive literary platform and willing to print "writers or books that the big companies are too money-hearted to print or too dumb to print."[83] Aside from Jessica Hagedorn, the book list at Momo's Press indeed provided an outlet for an eclectic set of writers such as Victor Hernandez Cruz, Ntozake Shange, Hilton Obenzinger, Beverley Dahlen, and Andrei Cordescu, among many others. In this interview, Reed calls Vincent's politics into question because of the fact that his recent article was about "Duncan and Jack Spicer and Allen Ginsberg and the same names" (78). Reed may have seen this as a limitation, but in fact, the kind of literary forum that Vincent was interested in creating was different from Reed's. It was one that placed equal weight and proportionate space for both white writers and minority avant-garde poets of merit rather than rendering them oppositional. As he explains, a "multicultural" literary platform that excluded white writers by default carried the risk of ultimately working to the disadvantage of minority writers:

> I wanted a variety of good writers from different backgrounds and aesthetics to appear in the same arena to explore what those contrasts would do to the language, as well as to reflect the larger social/political scope of the City by which we had begun to define ourselves. The books and magazine were quite successful. Unbeknownst to the mainly white-owned publishing industry, the Civil Rights movement, gay liberation, and feminism had begun to create a huge potential audience. Obviously, industry publishers began to figure that out by the 1980s and 1990s. Ironically, in contrast to my desire to collect good writing and writers as an *ensemble*—interesting because of its inherent conflicts and potential to create new work—the large publishers and institutions drove things in the direction of promoting "identity-centered" writing—black, Latino, and Asian. This often led to audience segmentation by race and, often, the aggrandizement of a kind of ghettoized writing. That did not interest me much.[84]

Shocks was so named as that which could absorb the series of shocks at a time of extreme social upheaval and political collision, a time punctuated in rapid succession by the assassinations of John and Robert Kennedy and Malcolm X, violent and murderous reactions against the civil rights movement, the constant televised horrors of the Vietnam War, on top of the ongoing ideological eruptions of the women's movement, gay rights, and the internal Third World liberation movement:

> As an editor and publisher of both *Shocks* and Momo's Press, I saw myself as a mender. *Shocks* were the reverberations I felt emanating

> from just about every writing quarter. The magazine and the press were a way of establishing a larger writing out of intense and conflicting fragments. The sum would be greater than the parts. It was time to break away from the focus on one writer over another, or the myth of the writer as isolated and independent hero. The intention became to establish contexts in which writers could occur in simultaneous situations. . . . The idea was to create a collective journal in which the various writings would vibrate off one another to create a larger dimension. This interfacing of borders and crossings of various writings and writers has remained the most serious intention of the press.[85]

Vincent's naming of his press after Momo, his grandmother who passed away in the 1960s, reflected the connective vision of his literary press, a perfect name as a medium sought to fill the gaps, silences, and absences from existing historiography:

> My grandmother was the child of emigrant Swedes in late 19th Century[,] farmers in northern California. (In Swedish "Momo" means "mother of mother"). My grandmother, who did not go beyond high school, loved to read. She could remember in the 1920s reading Fitzgerald in the magazines. I was always giving her novels from undergraduate and graduate reading lists, Kafka, Sherwood Anderson, Faulkner, James. Nothing fazed her interest. Impressive to me was my grandmother's capacity to articulate her photographic memory of her childhood in Humboldt County (Northern California). Histories of local Indians, vigilante hangings, the unpermitted stuff. This sense of taboo, or unveiling the veiled, evolved to implicitly become part of the publishing program of Momo's Press.[86]

Vincent's work as a publisher and editor was also influenced by a global purview that he had developed through his work in the Peace Corps during the mid-1960s. During his time teaching at the University of Nigeria, Nsukka, Vincent became involved there in an oral history project, and visited Ogoja Province on the Cameroon border, where he made tape recordings of local fables and cyclic songs of birth, naming, coming of age, marriage, and war, and funeral dirges, with the thought that "the farther a song can travel, the better."[87] Devastatingly, the two cassette tapes of these recordings actually got lost in the turmoil of having to leave in the midst of the mounting political tension in Nigeria leading up to Biafra in 1967, so that he was ultimately unable to bridge a deep global divide which he knew to exist: "The deep power the spoken or sung word still holds in contexts almost totally separate from technological contact" remained ever remote from the "media-saturated Westerner (or any modern urban dweller)." But the very knowledge of how physically far away these two worlds were, how disconnected they were from one another, and that they may never come into direct contact or be truly aware of the existence of one another also had to have shaped Vincent's continued role as a mediator once he came back to San Francisco, as an editor and publisher who prioritized his role in connecting worlds that the writers and poets can bring to life.

The concrete awareness Vincent had about the inability of the subaltern to speak would have made him different from much of Jessica Hagedorn's general audience in the mid-1970s. He was possibly among the small number of people who could accurately recognize and appreciate the unique sensibility and talent of another cosmopolitan subject straddling both sides of the global divide. At the very least, Vincent had an understanding of the particular class conflict that was shaped by the legacy of Western imperialisms that moved well beyond a simplistic fascination with her hybrid ethnic background (Spanish-Chinese-Scottish-Irish-French-Filipino).[88] In a 1982 letter written to the German critic and translator Günter Ohnemus, Vincent pins down the particular class tension at the heart of Hagedorn's writing: "She comes from a divided world—her father is one of the wealthier men in the Philippines, and her mother is a cook for one of the richest families in San Francisco/ Jessica is a mix of aristocratic grace and ethnic worker anger. When the writing is good, as it often is, the stuff burns!"[89]

Had Hagedorn taken interest in one of Vincent's suggestions about a possible book, there may have been a book that was not unlike Amitava Kumar's *Bombay–London–New York,* thirty years ahead of its time. In a letter dated April 3, 1979, as Hagedorn started working on her first revision of "Pet Food," Vincent throws out the following idea as an alternative:

> In the meantime, I think it is important that you get a new book out. I think it should be a mix of poems and travel journals. But *deep.* I think you shd [*sic*] look at that whole configuration
>
> Philippines—SF—New York—Europe—Jamaica
>
> find the thread (not in self-conscious stupid way) but some "gestalt" of pieces from each of those locations that add up. There's a search going on.[W]hat I'm suggesting is that cross between journals and poems might be the way into coming up with something

> solid/that would cast an even more powerful shape than *Dangerous Music.* (but again you might have something else in your satchel—a novel of that all, or a whole new series of poems/what can I say all I can really do is suggest)[90]

* * *

When Jessica Hagedorn submitted the first version of "Pet Food" to Stephen Vincent in 1976, she jokingly referred to it as "the oldest living legend of a novella anybody's ever heard of."[91] She had been working on the novella for five years by that time. But the speed with which she made two major rewrites before it was published in *Pet Food and Tropical Apparitions* was very quick. Her first rewrite drew from what she had turned into a play script, and it would take two major revisions before publication, with its final form substantially different from the original 1976 version of "Pet Food." An entire beginning section was cut, and several characters, scenes, and references were also eliminated, while new parts are added to develop the recognizable parts of the original plot, characters, and scenes. The novella emerges as a more linear work, and the character Boogie, in particular, developed more and more through these revisions. Many of these edited changes relied heavily on feedback and a series of suggestions made by Stephen Vincent, and to some degree by the novelist Keith Abbott. In what follows, I discuss two sets of comments Vincent made about the original 1976 manuscript as well as those he made for the two revisions Hagedorn submitted between 1979 and 1980.

In response to the original copy of the novella, Vincent sent a four-page handwritten note in 1978 that sketched out major and minor concerns about the opening of the original novella. On top of the first page, Vincent writes, "Beginning LARGE PROBLEM," followed farther down by an explanation:

> I find the first high school pages harsh in tone/I guess also disturbing is that novel leads off as if it's going to be *histoire* of relations among the women/and it isn't/so real energy does not get really until page 8.

Hagedorn agrees with this when she writes back on February 23, 1979:

> Boy, do I hate the first part! Not only does it sound harsh, it doesn't make much sense. Oh well, that's what happens when you write a novel over a five-year period, changing styles and concerns as you

go along. I think I'm gonna drop the whole first part. It's too much work to re-write that shit and make it mean something to ME.

On that first page, Vincent had also written, "too many characters," listing some of the characters that are weaker or need more attention. He returns to this point on the second page, where he lists the characters he finds compelling.

MOST POWERFUL:
a) Boogie
b) Parrot man/ and his quarters
c) Silver Daddy and family
d) Genji
e) Dr. T & Jerome

These are the characters that all stayed in the novella, while the characters he considered weak (Juliet of the Spirits, the Contessa, and Primo) were dropped. "You're right," she writes back, "my main concern is her relationship to Boogie, then her mama & non-existent papa, then her lovers. The rest of it is icing on a lopsided cake."

In January 1980, Vincent also sent Hagedorn an additional list of suggestions about what parts to incorporate from the play script version of "Pet Food." In these suggestions, Vincent advises her to incorporate new parts of the play script as a way of maximizing the impact of her writing, directing her to consider the effect of particularly powerful new sections that can serve to develop an interesting character, as well as amplify, foreshadow, or create a compelling tension within the key monologue/ scene that would follow later.

1) Use of Mom material from play: the first scene of play. As you leave home, in the novel, establish her nastiness towards what you value (James Dean, etc), as well as yr friends. Get the strength of her position in yr life established early, so that funeral exorcism will come off more powerful.

2) Moma Magenta from play into book (p eleven in Novel)/ bring her "practical honesty" or is it sardonic honesty & survival sense into book, as she foreshadows your meeting with Silver Daddy. (You might have to answer to why she is not around when you almost O.D. on Cinderella's "gift")

3) Let more of Stanley's take on artists (like the "flute" bit) in San Francisco from the play come into the novel as you take Paolo's room and/or when P dies.

> 4) Somehow the Father part from the first "George & Boogie" section has to be incorporated. Your dream of getting murdered before he does by the guerrillas.
>
> 5) & that, in turn, will get played against Genji's later speech, "How do you think it feels to be the bastard son of the Emperor"
>
> 6) I can't find at the instant the section in the novel where, if he does, Rover tempts her with the guitar, the white falcon, or is that only in the play. There should be such a concrete temptation with the music (via the guitar) so that the less amorphous as only a haunting figure.
>
> 7) The way Boogie opens up to George in the play at the end shd be incorporated: maybe on one of the visits to G at Dr. T's

Though the original manuscript is different from the published version, some sections of the novella's key moments remain almost completely the same: George's discovery of her new apartment, dinner at Silver Daddy's residence, his daughter Porno's disturbing monologue, correspondence between George and her father, and George's mother's monologue at Auntie Greta's funeral. This can be explained by Vincent's reply with the following letter, written in response to the first major revision:

> Hi Jessica,
>
> First apologies for the delay. I've been juggling from the revisions back to the original etc. & got an afternoon now where I've been handling both. Something struck me as off in the revised. I liked the added content about your mom, and the encounter w/ Moma Magenta. The encounter w/ Paolo in the room dance, almost there. But, to get to the point, the tone was off; lost connection with the power of the first manuscript. Tone: that cross between bad ass & Alice in Wonderland/ the abrupt switches between wonder & jab. The revisions lost the urgency. So I went back into the original, right from the start. First the intro sets up that A. Wonder motif/ tone. And then jumping the girl friends to page four, "My mother wanted to know why I smoked dope", then over to "Boogie in the Palace" (section) from there on with Silver Daddy and Paolo— it's all concrete (but dropping the characters who don't mount up as book progresses/ see I think each of those situations can be expanded to accommodate the material you cover in the revisions. Aunt Gretta can be in the scene with mother wanting to know why you smoked dope/ he can come in wanting to know where is chandeliers are—and fact she can't handle either one of you, but jealously needs you both to survive (whatever) that's the way to

> keep the snap in the language (the revisions slack off that tone/ it becomes too much picture book, almost nostalgia) where the young lady is actually on a search, throwing herself into the world, scary initiation risk.
>
> I know this must sound hellishly depressing. I feel partly responsible because I sense I said things that led in the more pictorial direction. But look it isn't to drop the images, it's just to get them to ripple off, jump up out of the natural process of her journey. So it's, what I'm suggesting, is diving back into the original, shedding the stuff that doesn't carry weight, and amplifying the stuff you keep with the new information (the early images we should get of Auntie G will in turn make the funeral more farcical etc). I sense part of the problem is jumping back into cathartic tone of first write/ which is different than the space you are in now (I think, maybe—but I am sure you still carry a lot of that with you & it's totally accessible). If it's a help, don't imagine what I am suggesting as something huge, & big re-write/ just a lot of shedding & some amplifying but maintain the tone that's the killer, your power- the way out of the various clutches/ at least the dangerous ones.
>
> (But Steve I've got a band, and to do this and that and this and how am I ever—Look if you do this it will carry you through 24 bands if you do this well it will carry you through.
>
> Honest.[92]

Having received "the revised, deluxe edition" of the novella Hagedorn sent in a month later, Stephen Vincent consulted the novelist Keith Abbott (hired for one hundred dollars) for his opinion of the suggestions made above. Based on Abbott's comments, Vincent makes further suggestions that determine important factors of "Pet Food" such as the opening, the introduction of Boogie early on through the aversion that George's mother has for him, and the incorporation of George's flashback to the Jimi Hendrix concert that she goes to with Boogie from the play script version, and the linearity of the narrative line in her second revision. The development of Boogie's presence is also a part of Vincent and Abbott's opinion that "the thing is to give more life so that George, as well as the rest of us, will reckon with a real loss at the end."[93]

The maintaining of tone, what Vincent called "the killer," remains important to the narrative construction of the novel to follow, *Dogeaters*, although the linearity of the narrative involving one main character does not become central until the second novel, *The Gangster of Love*. *Dogeaters* has two major narrative strands revolving around the main characters,

Rio (Gonzaga) and Joey Sands, but also has multiple narrative strands that all weave into one another. Working on stronger definition of characters and amplifying of scenes were also suggested by Hagedorn's editor at Penguin, Helena Franklin. In a letter dated February 1, 1989, Franklin starts by saying that "all the problems of the original draft" to which she seems to have alluded in an earlier letter (not found among the Jessica Hagedorn Papers) are solved: "Dolores and Isabel are now two very different women, Svero, Freddie and Ledesma all distinctly individual men. The torture scene is now very powerful indeed, and Daisy, I think, now 'works'—not as a flesh-and-blood woman but as a larger-than-life figure, which is just as good. She sort of embodies the legendary quality that the book deals with a lot, but in one of its positive forms. And I felt that the whole Lolita/Ledesma thing had come into much better focus." As with the writing of "Pet Food," Franklin put back some sections, writing that "many of the scenes I loved the first time I read the book I still preferred as they were in the earlier draft."[94]

Franklin's editing sometimes differs in nature from that of Vincent and Abbott, particularly in her suggestions for sanitizing characters. Franklin worries that the audience might be put off by some of the descriptions of the characters that prompt visceral reactions of repulsion:

> there were several places where material from the new draft seemed to emphasize physical grossness—people pigging out and belching, gross food, laxative-gobbling, barfing, etc.—in a way that risked serious over kill. I sense that this stuff expressed your gut reaction (forgive the pun) to all sorts of moral grossnesses, but it doesn't really convey that to the reader, who's apt to just go "yick" and switch off. You can use this sort of thing for shock value, but only sparingly—pretty soon it jut [*sic*] makes us *not* react to the shocks we need to. And it got so that you could tell a bad guy when he or she burped. So I did cut quite a lot of that.

Similarly, following Franklin's preference, the character General Ladesma became that of a "fastidious man" rather than a "sex pig":

> Generally, on the few occasions when someone in the book seemed to be doing or saying something out of character, I just queried you about it on a flag. This happened most with the General, since in the course of writing the second draft you seemed to abandon the idea of him as a "sex pig" (and I was pleased to see this!) in favor of a more complex portrait of a "fastidious" man who, though he was a torturer and a cheat, was also desperate to be respectable, didn't

> like drinking and drugs, didn't like women to talk dirty or mistresses to speak of wives, and wanted novenas said for him. I think that helped to differentiate him wonderfully from Severo, and increased the tension between him and Lolita. So I ended up questioning a burp here, a remark there, and many of the early "sex pig" references in the Tsismis section (on which more later).

That the sanitizing of the novel becomes important reflects what was necessary in marketing the novel to the general audience in the late 1980s. It may very well be that these changes contributed to the resounding success of *Dogeaters* as a novel, and perhaps it is a small concession. The dark humor of Hagedorn's stories remains in place. Still, it seems worth highlighting that the suggestions from Vincent and Abbott did not involve any sanitizing of Hagedorn's raw artistic vision. Vincent's own comment about a demand to do so is more telling than anything about the sympathy he felt for what shaped Hagedorn's early artistic vision: "In terms of eliminating or paling down the 'funk' in her work, I think that must have been hard for her to do—as a young teenager and adult I remember being much in love with Sly and The Family Stone, the Funkadelics and the musics spoke from 'the streets' in contradistinction the smoother sides of Motown. An attraction to the 'raw' materials."[95]

3 / L.A.–Paris–New York: The Parameters of Literary Production at the Turn of the Twenty-First Century

Starting in the 1970s and escalating with the financial deregulation of the 1980s and 1990s, the U.S. publishing industry went through a phenomenal shift as many traditionally independent publishing houses were subjected to mergers and restructuring, increasingly absorbed under transnational media conglomerates. The publishing houses were expected to yield the same kind of return of revenue brought in by other forms of media, three to four times more than what they had been making in the past. At the turn of the new century, the U.S. media industry at large was run by five corporate giants (Time Warner, Disney, Viacom, News Corp, and Bertelsmann, in that order).[1] In 2001, 80 percent of book sales were controlled by large publishing houses under foreign-based global capital: Random House (Germany), HarperCollins (Australia), St. Martin's/Macmillan (Germany), Thomson (Canada), Pearson (United Kingdom), and Houghton Mifflin (France). In different ways, editors and publishers were forced to negotiate this global change, whether at a small nonprofit literary press, a major literary publishing house, or a major commercial publishing house. This is why the critiques of globalization that emerged from these outlets are of particular interest, and I discuss multiple critical standpoints established by Asian American literary works that shed light on the urgent realities of the new global divide, the enduring legacy of former imperialisms at the heart of globalization, and the predatory nature of financialized capitalism that continues to expand the source of exploitation.

One insightful account of the publishing industry's shift into the global economy is André Schiffrin's *The Business of Books* (2000), in which the former Pantheon managing director argues that the neoliberal takeover of the publishing industry reflects an erosion of foundational democratic principles. Schiffrin invokes the debate over the privatization of radio during the 1930s, quoting from Robert McChesney's *Rich Media, Poor Democracy* (1999): "Freedom of speech is the very foundation of democracy. To allow private interests to monopolize the most powerful means of reaching the human mind is to destroy democracy. Without freedom of speech, without the honest presentation of facts by people whose primary interest is not profits, there can be no intelligent basis for the determination of public policy."[2] At a heightened moment of the book, Schiffrin narrates an executive meeting that turned into a standoff between himself and Alberto Vitale, the former banker from Italy who had become the head of the German conglomerate Bertelsmann's management team in the United States. Upon his takeover at Random House, where Pantheon had been an imprint since 1961, Vitale had told Schiffrin to cut Pantheon's list and staff by two-thirds. Schiffrin had responded by having the corporation's accountants draw up a budget that showed that such cuts would be far less profitable. The meeting for the spring 1990 list illustrates the kind of conflict that was playing out everywhere in the publishing industry:

> Vitale looked through the books that we were about to publish for spring 1990, a list we were particularly proud of. "Who is this Claude Simon?" he asked disdainfully, having clearly never heard of the Nobel Prize–winning novelist, "and this Carlo Ginzburg?" probably Italy's best-known historian. I then noticed that he would begin reading on the right side of the page, where the print runs were listed, and only then moved to the puzzling titles. For him, it was as if we were a shoe manufacturer, making sizes too small to fit most customers. "What is the sense of publishing books with such small printings?" he shouted. Were we not ashamed of ourselves? How could I face myself in the mirror each morning knowing that I wanted to publish such hopelessly unprofitable titles? The list included [Matt] Groening's books, which, according to our reckoning, would more than amply pay for the losses that might be incurred by the more difficult books. But Vitale's new policy was that each book should make money on its own and that one title should no longer be allowed to subsidize another. (90)

The characterization of Vitale's directive as more akin to "a plant closing than [to] the discussion of the future of a publishing house" aptly emphasizes the cold disinterest with which new corporate management regarded anything other than shareholder profit. It was indeed the very same drive behind the U.S. corporations that shut down manufacturing plants and outsourced the jobs to parts of Asia where labor is cheap and the workers' basic human rights are not guaranteed, resulting in the subsequent devastation of industrial cities in the United States as workers lost their manufacturing jobs. Vitale's inability to recognize a famed historian from his own country drives home the irony that a global management team (an Italian working for a German company in the United States) is unable to perceive the international edge that defined Pantheon: "Pantheon stood out for its cosmopolitanism—the degree to which it looked outside the United States for new and often dissenting ideas (65). Under Schiffrin's tenure as publisher, Pantheon had been a pioneer in introducing a body of influential works from Europe, including Michel Foucault, Günter Grass, Jean-Paul Sartre, Simone de Beauvoir, and Marguerite Duras, among many others (48–49).[3] Several weeks after the meeting, Schiffrin resigned along with a number of his senior editors at Pantheon when it became clear that they would be losing their jobs. Helena Franklin, Jessica Hagedorn's editor for *Dogeaters* at Penguin, was in fact one of the two other Pantheon editors who walked out in protest later in May.[4] Thus in the Jessica Hagedorn Papers, Franklin's letter from 1989 is typed on a letterhead from Pantheon, where *Dogeaters* was initially supposed to have been published.

Schiffrin's account attests to the fact that the debilitating aspects of the globalizing process were keenly felt by the editors and publishers who were committed foremost to the expansion of knowledge and aesthetic innovation:

> As one publishing house after another has been taken over by conglomerates, the owners insist that their new book arm bring in the kind of revenue their newspapers, cable television networks, and films do—businesses that have always enjoyed far higher profit margins. New targets have therefore been set in the range of 12–15 percent, three to four times what the publishing houses have made in the past. To meet these new expectations, publishers drastically change the nature of what they publish. (118–19)

A similar observation has been made by Allan Kornblum, the publisher of Coffee House Press, a small nonprofit press in Minneapolis that published Karen Tei Yamashita's *The Tropic of Orange*. In a 2009 interview, Kornblum shared his views about the impact of the demand produced by the monopolization of the publishing industry by foreign capital:

> In the 1980s and 1990s, bigger publishers began gobbling up smaller publishers, and then multinational corporations swallowed up the bigger publishers. Suddenly these houses needed to service the debt involved in buyouts, on top of the relatively modest six-to-eight percent return on investment that Bennett Cerf and Alfred Knopf had once been happy to receive.[P]ublishing isn't going to return 20% or even 15% on the dollar—it never has in the past, and I don't think it will in the future. I think all these changes that are making things difficult for the major houses provide an opening for smaller publishers.[5]

Further, Kornblum also noticed that specific constraints were now placed on editors at these major publishing houses ("They have to pay strict attention to the bottom line. So they can't take risks on a new author who's not guaranteed to make a hefty profit").[6] Major houses now had to turn to small nonprofit presses like his own to find new writers and give them a test run; if they garner some good reviews from the critics and develop a readership, the big houses might then offer to publish their next book.

Kornblum had built Coffee House Press in 1984, with a vision to publish "books that present the dreams and ambitions of people who have been underrepresented in published literature, books that help build a sense of community, and books that help to shape our national consciousness."[7] Coffee House Press introduced many works by important Asian American writers, including Frank Chin, Lawson Fusao Inada, R. Zamora Linmark, David Mura, Sun Yung Shin, Yuko Taniguchi, Wang Ping, Ed Bok Lee, U Sam Oeur, and Kao Kalia Yang. While Kornblum also published a resourceful anthology edited by M. Evelina Galang entitled *Screaming Monkeys: Critiques of Asian American Images*, his rationale for selecting works by Asian American writers was often based on innovation and literary experimentalism in their writing, challenging a common assumption that "writers of color are so intent on speaking for and/or to their particular communities, that rather than experiment with the latest literary techniques, they rely on simple story-telling."[8] Referring to the writing of Shin, Taniguchi, and Ping, Kornblum commented that these Asian American writers "speak through their art about seeing the world with double vision."[9]

Kornblum himself was an avant-garde poet studying with the St. Mark's Church Project in New York, who then moved to Iowa City during the early 1970s. He had initially been a part of the Iowa Writers' Workshop at the University of Iowa, but eventually formed the

Actualist Poetry movement, which defined itself against what he saw as the academically restrained mode of expression of the Writers' Workshop. The movement included such poets as Anselm Hollo, Darrell Gray, Ted Berrigan, Dave Morice, and Chuck Miller. Andrei Cordescu's the Bowel Movement was its offshoot.[10] Although less well known than L=A=N=G=U=A=G=E poetry, Actualism was closer to the Dadaist spirit of the New York School, and Ron Silliman referred to Actualism as "the New York School's western cousin."[11] Their subjects ranged from science (cell transplants, for instance) to the art of poetry, giving the contemporary reviewer a sense that their poems "rejoiced in the surprise element of daily life."[12] From 1973, Kornblum started publishing handset letterpress books and pamphlets from Toothpaste Press, which had evolved from a mimeographed magazine called "Toothpaste." Even after Kornblum moved to Minneapolis to form the nonprofit literary publishing house, he maintained interest in New York School poetry. He published *Nice to See You: Homage to Ted Berrigan*, edited by Anne Waldman, for instance, which included poems, stories, essays, and drawings by Berrigan's friends and students, and he also became the primary publisher for the New York poet Ron Padgett.

Minneapolis is home to three distinguished literary publishing houses: Coffee House Press, Graywolf Press, and Milkweed Press. These publishing houses have all received endowments from such institutions as the Cowles Media Foundation, McKnight Foundation, Jerome Foundation, and Bush Foundation, as well as funding from the Minnesota State Arts Board. There is also a host of local companies that give generously to the arts, as well as local organizations that are supportive of cultural activity, including Intermedia Arts, Lake Superior Writers, and the Loft Literary Center. As Kornblum sees it, the mission of Coffee House Press, as a nonprofit literary press, is to serve the public good by producing "books that celebrate imagination, innovation in the craft of writing, and the many authentic voices of the American experience."[13] While there is an advantage to independent presses, in that new ideas do not have to make their way through several levels of management or obtain approval from accounting and legal departments, Kornblum is careful not to underestimate the risks of a new initiative falling through:

> Publishing is one of those places where art and commerce meet, and a press that forgets to mind the store in the excitement of the moment, can lose the store, and hurt their authors and their readers in the process. Indies need to take advantage of their ability to be nimble, control the costs of new initiatives, and live up to the values

> that made the publishing industry the heart of the marketplace of ideas, and the expression of the yearnings of the heart.[14]

Karen Tei Yamashita sent her first novel, *Through the Arc of the Rainforest*, to Kornblum in the late 1980s at the suggestion of Alan Lau, the poet and editor of the Seattle-based Asian American community paper *International Examiner*. At the time, Asian American literature had not truly emerged in the mainstream trade book industry, and as Yamashita recalls, "there was no clear niche for what I did. It wasn't Asian American feminist literature; it wasn't magical realism; it wasn't science fiction."[15] Kornblum received Yamashita's manuscript with singular enthusiasm:

> In January 1989, Karen sent me a query letter along with a first chapter of a book she called *O Matacao*. That sample chapter introduced a Japanese man who promptly fell off a cliff. When the man awoke, a little ball was floating six inches in front of his head. And it turned out that the ball was going to be the narrator for much of the book. I was captivated immediately, and asked for the entire manuscript. I didn't hear from her. After a while, I actually dug out her query again, and sent another letter asking for the complete manuscript again—that's how much that sample chapter had impressed me. It finally arrived later that fall, and I brought it with me when we drove down to Iowa to visit my in-laws for Thanksgiving. On the way back to the Twin Cities, my wife took a turn at the wheel, and I started reading the manuscript. With every page, my excitement grew. I wanted to share the energy, and started reading aloud to my wife. I kept thinking about how much I had loved *V* by Thomas Pynchon, when I read it in high school, and I wondered how I had gotten so lucky to have a manuscript that great, sitting in my lap. After some editing and a title change, *Through the Arc of the Rain Forest* came out on our fall 1990 list, and we sold out of the first printing of 3,000 copies in the first three weeks. ("Coffee House Press Editors")

Kornblum remained committed to Yamashita's writing and continued to publish her subsequent works. Her third novel, *Tropic of Orange* (1997), was a response to her return to Los Angeles from Brazil, where she had lived for nine years. She found that Los Angeles in 1984 was no longer the "black/white city with a pocket of Japanese Americans" of the 1950s and 1960s she had grown up in. It had changed drastically; "now a Latin American city . . . it was mixed, cosmopolitan, with a Korean influx."[16] *Tropic of Orange* offered a new image of the city changed by the impact of globalization, adding a much-needed corrective to the existing representations of L.A. In the novel, one of the major characters, Buzzworm, is handed a map of the 1972 "gang territories" from Mike Davis's influential account of L.A.'s cultural history, *City of Quartz: Excavating the Future in Los Angeles* (1990). As Buzzworm puzzles over the discrepancy between the map and his lived experience of growing up in East L.A. and shakes his head, the narrator poses a question that is central to the novel:

> Even if it were true, whose territory was it anyway? Might as well show which police departments covered which beats; which kind of colored people (brown, black, yellow) lived where; which schools got which kids; which taxpayers were registered to vote; which houses were owned or rented; which businesses were self-employed; which corner liquor stores served which people; which houses were crack; which houses banging; which houses on welfare; which houses making more than twenty thou a year; which houses had young couples with children; which elderly; which people been in the neighborhood more than thirty years.[17]

Although intellectuals, news reporters, filmmakers, or those at institutions like universities or museums have traditionally been given the authority to construct and deconstruct the mythography of L.A., Yamashita's novel is interested in articulating the experiences of people actually living in the global city, mapping out the trajectories of crisscrossing lives that are impacted by the forces of late capitalism on a daily basis. As I discuss in my analysis, the multiple narrative strands of the novel coalesce most compellingly when readers learns to shift their attention away from the characters in the center to those in the margins, and notice the world to be populated by the silent laboring bodies of migrants and the dispossessed, produced and ignored by the dominating force of globalization.

Speaking in 2004, Allan Kornblum referred to Houghton Mifflin as a large publishing house whose "mission is to make money for shareholders first, and to serve literature second."[18] Indeed, since 2001, Houghton Mifflin had come under the ownership of Vivendi Universal, the French conglomerate notorious for the privatization of the water supply in developing nations.[19] Harold T. Miller, Houghton Mifflin's chairman and president until 1990, lamented this fate, calling the sale of the company "mysterious," with "reasons never publicly reported, and in turn, placed on the auction block in 2002." [20] In response, Miller took on the task of compiling interviews of people he identified as being representative of the original spirit of the company ("We were Boston and independent publishing"), characterizing their collective aspiration to have been, foremost, contributing to the shaping of "the nation's culture":

> Their academic degrees were in the liberal arts, and many of them could claim military experience with emphasis on discipline, leadership, and loyalty to one's unit and its people. They held to a sense of corporate memory reaching back to Henry Oscar Houghton's special interest in the authors his company published, a concern that overarched mere commercial considerations. Out of this commitment came an esprit de corps and sensitivity dedicated to the publication of books of value along with their pursuit of the innovative. They published books influenced more by a strong belief in the value of the book's content than its financials—the bottom line. (x)

Houghton Mifflin's publication of Asian American writing started much earlier than the discovery of Asian American writing as a profitable niche in the late 1980s. Harvard University's Houghton Library houses a formidable collection of their "blanks," records of every submission made to Houghton Mifflin headquarters in Boston, each consisting of the title, name of the author, a brief summary, and the rationale for the rejection. We do find among these "blanks" rejections of novels by Frank Chin and C. Y. Lee, which tells us that it was not necessarily easy for Asian American writers to be published by Houghton Mifflin. But as a publishing house that forged its identity as a reputable textbook publisher striving to provide "proper tools" for teachers, Houghton Mifflin was also among the first to respond to the need of new ethnic studies programs, and published Kai-Yu Hsu's *Asian American Authors* in 1970, which was the first anthology of Asian American literature with an Asian American editor. It was not until 1974 that Chin edited the *Yardbird Reader* (vol. 3) and *Aiiieeeee!*, by which point Houghton Mifflin had already started to explore the literary talent of Asian American writers, having published Bharati Mukherjee's *The Tiger's Daughter* (1972), and Ai's poetry collection *Cruelty* (1973). If Lawson Inada's *Before the War* was the first poetry collection to be published by a mainstream press (1971, William Morrow), Ai's collection had followed very closely.

Janet Silver, who published the Vietnamese American writer Monique Truong's *The Book of Salt*, arrived at Houghton Mifflin in 1984, with a background in literary studies of fiction and critical theory. She had served as a managing editor of *Critical Inquiry* for five years while working on her English PhD at the University of Chicago.[21] Her editorial work contributed to the moving of *Critical Inquiry* to the forefront in introducing major French theorists, and to the creation of a new space for emerging critical voices including Henry Louis Gates Jr.: "This was the heyday of the great deconstruction rage, so we were publishing the first translations of essays by Derrida, for instance, and Lacan, and some essays by Jacques Barzun. It was very, very intellectual. It was very abstract. But we were also publishing the early essays by people like Skip Gates."[22] Though it is difficult to track Silver's work, Elizabeth Abel credits Silver in the "Writing and Sexual Difference" issue, naming her, "if not in titlecoeditor of this issue."[23] Once at Houghton Mifflin, Silver worked on Margaret Atwood's *The Handmaid's Tale* and also handled works by Philip Roth, Tim O'Brien, Cynthia Ozick, Robert Stone, John Edgar Wideman, and Jonathan Safran Foer. In 1997, she became Houghton Mifflin's vice president, having become a senior editor in 1993 and been promoted to executive editor of adult trade books in 1995.

Silver took advantage of her position as vice president to introduce little-known writers. Notably, she made use of paperback originals, once considered appropriate only for genre fiction and largely ignored by reviewers, as a format that allows for publishing experimentation.[24] One such success, for instance, was the publication of Jhumpa Lahiri's celebrated short-story collection *The Interpreter of Maladies* (1999), which sold 40,000 copies that year and was followed up with a second printing of 75,000 copies.[25] She also expanded Houghton Mifflin's list to include other Asian American writers with interesting global perspectives, such as Anita Desai and Peter Ho Davies. Silver has said that she felt ambition for her writers rather than for herself. Having observed that the publishing world and the readership were changing and evolving, her successful work as editor involved recognizing that there was room for more books by women and ethnic writers, writing about "a certain kind of community and experience that wasn't very well represented." Silver weathered the storms of restructuring when Houghton Mifflin merged with Vivendi Universal in 2001, which was then sold to U.S. private equity firms Blackstone Group, Bain Capital, and Thomas H. Lee Partners the following year, and taken over by the Irish firm Riverdeep in 2006. When Houghton Mifflin merged with Harcourt in 2008, however, it was all but gutted, and Silver's position was eliminated.

During her tenure as vice president at Houghton Mifflin, Silver won the bid to publish Monique Truong's *The Book of Salt* (2003). Through a narrative about a Vietnamese cook serving Gertrude Stein and Alice B. Toklas in Paris, Truong's novel identifies a legacy of former Western imperialisms in the nascent stages of a U.S.-led global capitalism. Like Yamashita's novel, Truong's work gives voice to the normally silenced global migrant, here identified as the imperial subaltern to be resubjugated under late capitalism. As Truong explained in an interview, the inspiration for *The Book of Salt* came from reading Alice B. Toklas's cookbook, in which Toklas discusses her Vietnamese hired help:

> In a chapter called "Servants in France," Toklas wrote about two Indochinese men who cooked for Toklas and Stein at 27 rue de Fleurus and at their summer house in Bilignin. . . . I was, to say the least, surprised and touched to see a Vietnamese presence—and such an intimate one at that—in the lives of these two women. These cooks must have seen everything, I thought. But in the official history of the Lost Generation, the Paris of Gertrude Stein and Alice B. Toklas, these Indochinese cooks were just a minor footnote. There could be a personal epic embedded inside that footnote, I thought. *The Book of Salt* is that story, as told from the perspective of Bình, a twenty-six-year-old Vietnamese man living in Paris in the late 1920s. I have imagined him as one of the candidates who answered Stein and Toklas's classified ad. (press release, *The Book of Salt*)

By turning to the perspective of the Indochinese cooks, Truong's narrative challenges the conventional placement of the (white) modern bourgeois subject at the center of the Western novel, as well as the structural violence that renders less privileged human beings vulnerable to marginalization and silencing, turned into a "mere footnote." Bình's story in *The Book of Salt* is indeed epic, told in an intoxicatingly eloquent voice as articulated by Truong. Prior to Silver's acquisition of this novel, Truong had confronted a different editor, who raised objections to Bình's voice. How could a common laborer use the kind of sophisticated language that Bình speaks? She had expected that there would be, during the course of the novel, a story that explained how the narrator and protagonist Bình in Monique Truong's *The Book of Salt* came to speak so well.[26] This may seem like a reasonable question, but it exposes an assumption that one cannot possess an ardent mind, or cannot righly occupy the center of the novel, unless he or she achieves middle-class status. Actually, since Bình is known to speak very little English, like Stein's actual cooks, for the narrative itself to be told in English at all is already an impossibility. The way that the novel stretches the limit of what is possible, giving speech to the subaltern who cannot—as Gayatri Spivak was right to point out—speak, is precisely what is striking about Truong's narrative imagination.

The kind of corporate restructuring of the 1990s that so impacted the scene of literary production—prompting Vitale's behavior at Pantheon Books as well as the elimination of Silver's position at Houghton Mifflin—is of course intimately connected to the workings of the financial sector. In her anthropological exposé of Wall Street, *Liquidated: An Ethnography of Wall Street* (2009), Karen Ho unpacks the central role of Wall Street in the activities of corporate mergers and acquisitions including leveraged buyouts, as well as restructuring and downsizing:

> As financial advisors to major U.S. corporations as well as expert evaluators of and spokespeople for the stock and bond markets, investment bankers work to transfer and exchange wealth from corporations to large shareholders (and their financial advisors), hold corporations accountable for behavior and values that generate short-term shareholder value, and generate debt and securities capital to fund these practices. [. . .] The work of Wall Street does not consist only of trading and exchange in global financial markets; it is also linked to corporate restructurings and attendant shifts in corporate values.[27]

As Ho notes, Wall Street was substantially responsible for shaping the ways in which corporations shifted from the stable social institution of post–World War II welfare capitalism, which sought to make profit from proffered goods and services, into a much more volatile one of financialized capitalism, which is primarily concerned with raising shareholder value: "the increase of their stock prices for the benefit of the 'true owners,' the shareholders" (3). No longer does the profit of a corporation benefit employees; rather, that profit is often obtained at the *cost* of those same employees, since one of the easiest ways of achieving the short-term increase of shareholder value involves restructuring and downsizing. Ho reminds us that Wall Street itself also stood to gain from the conglomeration of the corporate world. Having depleted many of its staple revenue-generating tools during the 1970s, such as underwriting, investment banks had turned to mergers and acquisitions, encouraging senior executives to use their profit margin to buy unrelated companies. In their 1987 study of mergers and acquisitions *Mergers, Sell-Offs, and Economic Efficiency*, David J. Ravenscraft and F. M. Scherer exposed as false the claim that mergers and acquisitions resulted in increased profitability and efficiency, stating that "companies actually declined in productivity and synergies anticipated from acquisition frequently did not materialize."[28] Still, as Ho explains, investment bankers made hefty advisory and commission fees as well as a percentage cut of any other fund raising needed to enable the deal anyway, and the senior executives profited as well, with CEO salaries (many with stock options) rising to more than four hundred times that of the average worker by the end of 1980s.

The critique of Wall Street in Min Jin Lee's *Free Food for Millionaires* (2007), a novel about a Korean American girl named Casey Han who tries to make her way in Wall Street after graduating from Princeton in 1992, resonates strongly with Ho's critical approach in *Liquidated.* Ho used her institutional connections as a graduate student at Princeton in real life to be recruited into Wall Street to conduct fieldwork between 1996 and 1999. While *Liquidated* offers an appropriately detailed street-level vision of Wall Street, the effect of dramatization in the financial sector in Lee's novel is similar in defying the high-level abstraction in many authoritative discussions of global capitalism. *Free Food for Millionaires* chronicles the inner workings of Wall Street, from the exclusive recruiting process at elite institutions like Princeton and Harvard; the white-collar assembly line abuzz on the trading floor; the strategic spatial politics of office floors, the internal division within investment banks consisting of interns, office assistants, equity salesmen, sales division managers, analysts, and managing directors; hardworking brokers dining on the clients' dime. Lee exposes, as Ho does in *Liquidated,* "the daily practices and corporate cultural values of investment bankers in the workplace as the site which links the cultural frame, dispositions, and habitus of investment bankers with broader U.S. corporate restructuring and the construction of financial market boom and busts (Bourdieu 1990)." In the rejection of the god-like and disembodied bird's-eye-view, Lee's novel powerfully destabilizes what Ho's work seeks to challenge as well: "assumptions of a singular, static, totalizing capitalist worldview, promulgated by homogeneous capitalists" (29).

Free Food for Millionaires was a commercial success, appearing on the best-seller list in the *Boston Globe* and the "Best of 2007" list in the *San Francisco Chronicle.* It was featured in a favorable light in mainstream newspaper and popular magazine outlets including the *New York Times, USA Today, Wall Street Journal, New York Daily News, New York Times Book Review, Washington Times, Entertainment Weekly, SELF,* and *People,* as well as the more industry-targeted outlets like *Publishers Weekly* and *Booklist.* Some of this success might be attributed to the work of Lee's editor, Amy Einhorn, at Grand Central Publishing, whose commitment to thorough editing and exuberant salesmanship has previously been noted.[29] At a time when not all editors contribute to the editing process, Einhorn sees herself as a kind of publisher/editor who is "incredibly hands on—about everything—covers, flap copy, securing quotes, soliciting booksellers, the list goes on and on. . . . [A] major difference is probably that I edit everything I publish."[30] Lee herself recalls Einhorn as having been respectful of her creative vision: "The manuscript did not change materially in plot or language. It was edited, but I didn't feel like it was in any way problematic."[31] Still, the final manuscript was Lee's seventh version and went through four total rewrites after it was accepted.[32]

It is worth underscoring that unlike the novels by Yamashita or Truong, Lee's novel was published from an outlet that built itself on a commercial model. Grand Central Publishing was called Warner Books until 2007, and originated from the successful mass-market paperback publisher Paperback Library, acquired by Warner Communications in 1970, which then expanded with the acquisition of Popular Library in 1982. As Janice Radway explains in *Reading the Romance* (1984), Warner had followed the lead of Harlequin in pursuing commercial success of the popular fiction market like Fawcett and Dell, by "presenting romances as products in a specially designed series or line."[33] In Einhorn's words, "If you're at Warner, which was a great commercial house, and you get in a very literary novel, you likely won't do as well with it as if you were publishing it somewhere else."[34] During the 1990s and early 2000s, Einhorn had become a key player in commercial publishing, having worked for Simon and Schuster's Pocket Books before working at Warner Books, where she also helped develop the "5 Spot" imprint specializing in chick lit. Einhorn's talent as an editor at Warner is apparent in a slew of best sellers including Lolly Winston's *Good Grief* (2004), Robert Hicks's *The Widow of the South* (2005), Susan Jane Gilman's *Hypocrite in a Pouffy White Dress* (2005), and Amy Sedaris's *I Like You* (2006). Einhorn would go on to have an eponymous imprint at G. P. Putnam's Sons (owned by Penguin), where she edited *The Help* (2007) by Kathryn Stockett, a novel that sold 10 million copies, according to the official website.[35]

Though Einhorn's publishing career seems relatively unscathed by the global restructuring, it does involve a narrow escape from the impact of conglomerate management, which happened when Poseidon Press was merged into Simon and Schuster's adult division in 1993. The *New York Times* reported the shuttering of Poseidon Press as "another ominous step in the consolidation of Simon & Schuster's disparate publishing niches by the company's parents, Paramount Publishing and Paramount Communications, in the name of a more efficient bottom line. Other Simon & Schuster imprints that have fallen by the wayside in recent years include Summit Books, Linden Press and the trade division of Prentice Hall," quoting one high-ranking Simon and Schuster employee as saying, "I don't know what kind of commitment men sitting around in Los Angeles making movies have to the future of literature."[36] As Einhorn narrates this moment: "One day I came back from vacation and everyone had been fired except for me—they forgot I existed. So I went to Pocket, and then I was at Warner Books, which were both very commercial."[37]

It would be wrong to assume that success with a mainstream audience necessarily involves artistic compromise for an Asian American writer, as has been suggested in the past.[38] It is true that not all Asian American writers are invested in sociocultural critique (or have to be), as Yoonmee Chang has pointed out in *Writing the Ghetto: Class, Authorship, and the Ethnic Enclave* (2010), but some writers do participate in cultural negotiation, even within the given set of conventions that define popular fiction. Through exaggerated performance of established conventions, for instance, writers can reveal social codes embedded within formulaic fiction. Christopher Shinn writes about acclaimed Asian American writers shifting to the realm of thriller and occult in the mid-1990s precisely because popular mainstream cultural representation is "where exotic racist stereotypes frequently abound."[39] In that context, the 1989 publication of Amy Tan's *The Joy Luck Club*, which spent eight months on the *New York Times* best-seller list, is significant because it opened the doors of popular literature for Asian American writers. In the case of Amitav Ghosh, Lisa See, and Gus Lee, Asian American writers exploit the rules of pulp fiction, such as "elaborate plots, patently formulaic devices, and what we might call ethnic typologies" in order to effectively dramatize "the scaffolding of ethnic subjects in pursuit of social equality, law, order, and economic rationality, rendering grotesque an invisible global network of discipline that enacts violence akin to the torturing of the body."[40]

In *Free Food for Millionaires,* the critique of Wall Street borrows from the conventions of chick lit in its central narrative. Pamela Thoma argues in her analysis of Asian American women's popular fiction, *Asian American Women's Popular Literature: Feminizing Genres and Neoliberal Belonging* (2013), that chick-lit novels like Michelle Yu and Blossom Kan's *China Dolls* (2007) and Sonia Singh's *Goddess for Hire* (2004) use repetition and satire to "comment on the model of the citizen as a romantic consumer and disclose that for Asian American women in particular it requires prodigious material and affective labor."[41] In the case of Lee's novel, the staging of chick lit in the investment banking world is particularly fitting because Wall Street lies at the heart of conspicuous consumption and credit-card woes, which are common chick-lit tropes. The dramatic proliferation of credit cards since the 1980s could not have happened without the help of Wall Street, which has since devised highly sophisticated tools to turn consumer debt into a commodity from which to boost Wall Street investors' assets, through the financial alchemy of securitization.[42] The "true" beneficiaries of a consumer-driven economy are not all who work in the retail industry, for instance, but its select senior executives, shareholders, and investors, who are poised to enlarge their equity by keeping consumers in perpetual credit card debt.

As Saskia Sassen recently argued about the current state of financialized capitalism, "one of the last frontiers for financial extraction is modest-income households, of which there are a billion or more worldwide, and bail-outs through taxpayers' money."[43] This means that many middle-class subjects ensnared into conspicuous consumption and credit-card debt, a group that includes the readers of mass fiction, are also exploited by late capitalism in ways they had never been before. In my discussion of *Free Food for Millionaires* to follow, I show that the novel is sympathetic to the mass audience who has increasingly started to shoulder the burden of globalized economy, but I also point out that the novel is not simply a two-dimensional or formulaic "opiate for the masses." Drawing from Edith Wharton's *The House of Mirth*, Lee's novel maintains a certain critical distance from the central chick-lit narrative, raising questions about the values and practices of people in Wall Street who are a part of it. While it is difficult to discern how invested Einhorn was in the social critique of Lee's novel, the intertextuality between *The House of Mirth* and *Free Food for Millionaires* had to have appealed to the editor who looks for what she calls "the sweet spot between literary and commercial." Finding that balance is "what she does best," as she said in a recent interview. She has since left her imprint at G. P. Putnam to take up a new position as vice president at Flatiron (Macmillan), following the merger of historic proportions between Penguin and Random House in July 2013.[44]

Animating the Global South in Karen Tei Yamashita's *Tropic of Orange* (1998)

In Mike Davis's *City of Quartz,* a photograph of bagged oranges left stacked one on top of another on a graffittied sidewalk as garbage to be collected is emblematic of excess and waste, reinforcing the feeling that Los Angeles is "a stand-in for capitalism in general."[45] In *Tropic of Orange*, these oranges would become a central metaphor for the silenced voices in global circulation, metonymic of all other "gifts from NAFTA" (North American Free Trade Agreement) that she lists: "Oranges, bananas, corn, lettuce, guarachis, women's apparel, tennis shoes, radios, electrodomestics, live-in domestics, living domestics, gardeners, dishwashers, waiters, masons, ditch diggers, migrants, pickers, packers, braceros, refugees, centroamericanos, wetbacks, wops, undocumenteds, illegals, aliens" (163). In Yamashita's remarkable use of the list, the oranges slowly transform into laboring human beings in global circulation, silenced, denigrated, and othered to be policed.

Yamashita's *Tropic of Orange* itself begins with an image of one particular orange that grows near Mazatlán in Mexico. The orange tree itself grows on the Tropic of Cancer that runs through the property belonging to one of the major characters, Gabriel Balboa. Rafaela Cortes, who is hired to look after the house as she figures out what to do with her troubled marriage, had noticed an imaginary line emanating from the navel orange tree's "tiny bud":

> a line—finer than the thread of a spiderweb—pulled with delicate tautness. . . . Perhaps it was something like a thin laser beam or light passing through an optic fiber. Rafaela was not sure. She knew that it ran across Gabriel's property. In fact, she sensed that it continued farther in both directions, east and west, east across the highway and west toward the ocean and beyond. (12)

When the flower bears fruit, she notices that the "baby orange . . . seemed to grasp that line as its parent," which rocks back and forth in the wind with "the growing orange . . . like a lullaby." Rafaela enjoys watching "the transition of its small growing globe, first from green and then to its slow golden burnish," which quenches her desire to see "a thing out of season struggle despite everything and become whole" (12). The Tropic of Cancer, an imaginary line that happens to roughly coincide with the border that separates the global South from the global North, is used here as a spatial metaphor of the global divide that is "as wide as an entire culture and as deep as the social and economic construct that nobody knew how to change" (256). The orange is a hopeful image at the borderlands that Gloria Anzaldúa called "*una herida abierta*, where the Third World grates against the first and bleeds."[46]

As though it were a character in its own right, the orange stays in the narrative throughout the book, which takes it north toward "The Village of the Reign of the Angels of Porciuncula, the second largest city of Mexico, also known as Los Angeles" (212). There is no reason why the orange cannot be treated as a character. It is a living thing, and even if we perceive no signs of a distinctive interiority or intellect, its two-dimensionality is no different from that of plenty of minor characters populating the margins of almost any given novel. *Tropic of Orange* begins with this orange falling from the tree, stopping "just beyond the frontiers of Gabriel's property to a neutral place between ownership and the highway" (13). It ends up in a local marketplace where it is picked up by yet another major character, the mythical performance artist Arcangel, who had a dream vision about this very same orange: "*a woman was pushing a cartalong a highway / toward the city, / only to come upon an orange, / out of season, / there along that horizontal line / where the sun sliced the tropics. / she stooped, / scooped the thing up, / threw it in the cart with the cactus and shrugged*" (71). The orange travels inside Arcangel's suitcase as he takes a bus north. Rafaela will later reencounter the orange: "Rafaela knew the orange as she knew the face of her child. The strands of the line extended from two ends of the orange, reaching out of the suitcase, tangling about Arcangel, and slipping across the bus, through the windows, and across the land" (154). When Arcangel reaches the U.S.–Mexico border, his orange becomes emblazoned with images of "hundreds of thousands of unemployed" that "surged forward—the blessings of monetary devaluation that thankfully wiped out those nasty international trade deficits" (201):

> *Then came the kids selling Kleenex and Chiclets*
> *the women pressing rubber soles into tennis shoes,*
> *the men welding fenders to station wagons and*
> *all the people who do the work of machines: human washing machines,*
> *human vacuums,*
> *human garbage disposals.*
> . . . .
> *everything and everybody got into lines—*
> *citizens and aliens—*
> *the great undocumented foment,*
> *the Third World War,*
> *the gliding wings of a dream.* (201)

The orange also comes to embody the persecuted global migrants who are already in L.A. When Arcangel and others arrive in L.A., there are no other oranges in sight. Earlier in the week, two men in a red convertible Porsche had been heading north toward Hollywood "peeling oranges, bouncing flippant ideas for a storyboard back and forth," when the driver passed out for unknown reasons at the wheel, causing a massive accident on the freeway, "spread across ten lanes, hundreds of cars piled one onto the other" so that it was blocked for days (55). Attributing the cause to the orange, the media first reported a "spiked orange alert" which has FDA investigators, local Health Department inspectors, and FBI agents working around the clock (139). "The spiked orange alert" turned into "illegal orange scare," in which "every peddler in the orange business was seeing his merchandise confiscated at gunpoint" (140). It then escalated into an "illegal *alien* orange scare," targeting imported oranges that may include an "unidentified natural hallucinogen plus traces of rare tropical snake venom. You got high, saw god, and got killed" (141). Ultimately the orange is hyped as "*death* oranges":

> Oranges went underground. The word was emphatic: All oranges were suspect. And deemed highly toxic. Waste companies hauled the rotting stuff by the tons to landfills. Environmental experts declared them toxic waste. Sniff the chalky fungus and you could be dead fast. The poison could leach into the water system. Fruit flies could spread it too. County Ag Inspector Richard Iizuka said it loud and clear: See an orange? Call 911. Minute Maid doesn't skip a beat in announcing a switch over to Passion Fruit, which is relayed immediately by a Talk Show host on TV: "Passion fruit is all the rage. Minute Maid is selling under the trade name, *Passion.*™ Make the change now." (142)

The paranoia that prompts an immediate and absolute ban on oranges resonates with the social realities of transnational migrant workers being perpetually criminalized and forced to go back and forth on the border. As Arjun Appadurai remarks in *Modernity at Large*, the rhetoric of numbers in Western modernity has the ability to turn the complex historical conditions of these subjects into entities who are enumerated and abstracted. Shorn of interiority, they are shaped into "global traffic":[47]

> *its great history of migrations back and forth—in recent history,*
> *the deportation of 400,000 Mexican*
> *citizens in 1932,*
> *coaxing back of 2.2 million*
> *braceros in 1942*
> *only to exile the same 2.2 million*
> *wetbacks in 1953.* (198)

By turning the orange into a character despite its inability to speak, and having the orange stand in for the entire global South, *Tropic of Orange* counters a major structural violence implicit in the Western novel: the production of the main figure's centrality through the marginalization and silencing of the many.

Gabriel, Rafaela, and Arcangel are characters around whom three of the seven major narrative strands in the novel forcefully cohere into a vision of L.A. At first, it seems as though the narrative revolving around

Gabriel, the Chicano newspaper reporter handling local news and a film noir aficionado, is central to the novel. His is the only first-person narrative in the novel, which creates an identification with the character that feels closer in proximity than the rest of the narratives, which are told in third person. In the beginning, the reader has to make sense of the six other characters, who don't always seem related to one another, through their relationship to Gabriel. Emi Sakai is his on-and-off girlfriend, Rafaela Cortes and Bobby Ngu run a janitorial service at Gabriel's office, and Buzzworm is his inner-city "connection" who lets him know if there's any "story" worth pursuing. Manzanar Murakami is one of the (rejected) leads that Buzzworm had given him. Arcangel, a mythical personification of the folk hero in the global South, is a man whom Rafaela meets at Gabriel's ranch in Mexico, a little north of Mazatlán. However, Gabriel's centrality starts to lose ground as the novel progresses, for each of the narrative strands starts to develop in seemingly every which way. The limitedness of Gabriel's singular narrative vision, which for all intents and purposes is an approximation of the bourgeois white male subject, is further underscored by the variety and range of the omniscient third-person narrator in this novel. The narrative strands belong to different genres, from realism (Gabriel, Emi, and Bobby) to surrealism (Arcangel), and different shades of magical realism somewhere in between (Rafaela, Buzzworm, and Manzanar). At a certain point, Gabriel's narrative starts to stray away from those of the other characters, and stops being useful in explaining what is taking place in the trajectory of the novel as a whole. Gabriel's narrative takes him away from L.A. into Mexico as he pursues a wild-goose chase of a narcotics-related case, and although he does end up saving a Mexican village in the end, he is entirely absent from the spectacular final showdown between the beneficiaries of global capitalism ("Super NAFTA") and the people of the Global South ("El Gran Mojado"). When the reader is able to let go of Gabriel's story and the conventions of realism that belong to his narrative, paying closer attention to the stories that seemed less important than his at first, the novel starts to yield to a vision of the world that is being reshaped in different ways by the forces of late capitalism.

To a large extent, Gabriel's centrality is destabilized almost from the start by his girlfriend Emi. Her sophisticated mastery of the dizzyingly cutting-edge technology and *au courant* social trends in the global city makes Gabriel's perspective seem outdated and quaint, or more or less irrelevant. From "doing the Joan Didion freeway thang" in her black Toyota Supra (58) and helping Gabriel get to LAX along the way, to her expert navigation in cyberspace, which ultimately helps Gabriel save a

Mexican village toward the end of the novel, Emi's mobility far exceeds Gabriel's own in speed and mileage. To Emi, Gabriel's "film noir stuff" is as passé as the *Pappardelli con fungi al vino marsala* on the menu will become next week (22), and with her fine-tuned sensibility, Emi can brutally dismantle the now classic images of film noir to which Gabriel is sentimentally attached. Emi exposes film noir's powerful images of L.A. as dark dystopia to be nothing more than a fiction of itself created by the capital of the world's Culture Industry, where mass culture is produced and corporate advertisements are steadily fed to consumers across the nation. She should know, as her job entails snipping TV programs, speeding them up electronically in order to insert advertisements for corporate sponsors, and stitching them all together without losing the integrity of the show.

When we first meet Emi, she bluntly points out to Gabriel that it never rains in L.A., and that "the only reason it rains in those films is so Bogie can wear a trenchcoat." In the next scene, she similarly protests that "Orchids don't smell. They don't overwhelm you with a languid trop-i-cal perfuuume [*sic*]. Have you ever heard of orchid sachet? Fragrance de Catalya?" (124). Even Raymond Chandler's classic detective hero Philip Marlowe is not safe from Emi:

> "It's not like I'm not interested in your habit. I mean this Philip Morris—"
>
> "Marlowe."
>
> "—Marlowe guy could have a revival. Then okay. But otherwise, strictly current affairs pour moi." (22)

Though the banter seems innocent enough, the slippage between Philip Marlowe and Philip Morris is actually disturbing because the interchangeability of these names suggests that Philip Morris has registered to Emi's mind as a kind of character rather than a corporation. Philip Morris, the transnational corporation that sports the imperialistic phrase "veni, vidi, vici" as its logo, is potentially much more predatory and dangerous than Chandler's hardboiled detective can ever be. If Philip Morris is a character, it is not so much a hero as a cyborg, dictated as it would be by the unyielding drive of global capitalism and seeking an ever-increasing margin of profit at the cost of eroding social mechanisms that protect basic human rights. Yamashita's novel easily anticipates the *Citizens United v. Federal Election Commission* ruling in 2010, if not the legal proceedings that Philip Morris International filed against the Australian government in 2012, in which the multinational corporation cites the investor-state dispute clause of the 1993 bilateral investment treaty between the governments of Australia and Hong Kong in order to launch a legal lawsuit against the Australian government, alleging that the proposed Australian laws for plain packaging would prevent them from making projected profit.[48]

What is troubling about Emi's *strictly-current-affairs-pour-moi* attitude that blends in with the chic Hollywood crowd hanging out at the "very center of Westside power plays" (21),[49] is that it is a disavowal of anything that has to do with the past and involves a disavowal of her connection to Asian American history and community. The "Asian princess" and "Judge Ito's smart-assed sister" (165) is among the highly educated generation of Japanese Americans who could be incorporated into the "mainstream" as a privileged figure embraced by the American middle-class brand of multiculturalism, although she herself complains of feeling "invisible" and "hate[s] being multicultural" (128). She feels herself to be so "distant from the Asian female stereotype" that "it was questionable if she even had an identity" (19), and if she chose to embrace her "ethnic" identity, it seems that this has to involve traveling to Japan. "Do you know what a ticket to Japan costs?" she asks Gabriel, "Dollar to yen dropped again. Do you know what a cup of coffee at Narita goes for? If I had the urge, do I have the financial backing to even get close to my roots?" (165). What she would find in Japan, of course, would not be the country that her family had left three generations ago, but another advanced postindustrial nation with its own set of the global elite. When she insists that there *is* such a thing as a non-Western flower without "languid trop-i-cal perfuume," these moments also indicate a refusal to be grouped together with the dark double to the Asian global "citizen": the racialized Asian working-class global migrant laborers in the United States. As a part of the culture industry, she is not on the side of those who are exploited by late capitalism, but on the side that perpetuates an exploitative structure even if that is done unwittingly.

Like Jessica Hagedorn's George, Emi assumes the traditionally male-coded role of the modern hero whose identity is defined by the disavowal of the past. However, unlike Hagedorn's novella, which assigns guilt rather than denouncing this figure altogether, Yamashita's Emi dies in the midst of one of the most chaotic moments toward the end of the novel, hit by a stray bullet. Emi's death turns the freeway into a hyperbolic spectacle that invokes Nathanial West's *The Day of the Locust* (1939), ending dramatically with her body literally ascending into heaven lifted up by the *NewsNow* helicopter, "requisitioned to save its own" (257). It is unclear who fired (and missed) the shot toward the satellite dish of her van, and in her last moments, Emi compares herself to the chauffeur in

Raymond Chandler's classic L.A. noir *The Big Sleep*, whose death is unexplained: "Someone asks the question: Who killed him? Script continuity, see. Nobody knows. They call up Raymond Chandler. He doesn't know either.Just because you get to the end doesn't mean you know what happened" (254). What we do know is that her death highlights the importance of the remaining narrative strands of the novel, which provide an equally important, if not more urgent, critical perspective from people who are marginalized by the capitalist global structure, in many ways dealing with issues that arise from being reduced to laboring bodies of global migration and nonskilled service sector labor. Instead of a narrative in which the cosmopolitan global subject emerges simultaneously at the cost of displacing underprivileged global migrant, as George Sand in Jessica Hagedorn's "Pet Food" does with Boogie, the cosmopolitan global subject is the one who is killed off in Yamashita's novel so that the global migrants can emerge from darkness.

Emi's death prompts us to reevaluate characters who might have appeared to be less important to the novel, which is now left with the other Asian character, Bobby Ngu, who runs a janitorial business with his wife, Rafaela. A Chinese man from Singapore with a Vietnamese name, living in L.A.'s Koreatown, Bobby has actually lived a remarkable survival story, narrowly escaping becoming a part of the collateral damage caused by global capitalism:

> Used to be, back in Singapore, Bobby had it easy. Dad had a factory. Putting out bicycles. Had a good life. Good money. Only had to go to school. One day American bicycle company put up a factory. Workers all went over there. New machines. Paid fifty cents more. Pretty soon, American company's selling all over. Exporting. Bicycles go to Hong Kong. Go to Thailand. To India. To Japan. To Taiwan. Bobby's dad losing business. Can't compete. That's it. (17)

As Bobby's story shows us, offshore industrial production, in which U.S.-based multinational corporations reap profit by using cheap labor from Asia, does not only mean that there is a sharp decline of manufacturing in the United States, or that small retail businesses in the United States are subsequently pushed out because they can't compete with the lower retail prices that offshore production allows, yielding to a monopolized market. In the very countries where manufacturing has moved its production, local manufacturing businesses also suffer because the transnational corporations can offer slightly higher wages.

Bobby's narrative strand also introduces us to illegal trade stemming from globalization. Having come to the United States under an assumed

Vietnamese name, Bobby has since successfully built a small business of his own and raised his younger brother, who is now in college, while sending back money to his father and two sisters in Singapore. He now owns a home in Koreatown and has married a woman from Mexico (Rafaela). The novel opens with his realization that Rafaela has left home with their son, Sol, but he also receives a letter from a "cousin from Hong Tian in Fujian, same village as his mother's father" (76), who needs his help in coming to the United States. One of the most intense moments in Bobby's narrative is the negotiation with the Snakehead from Chinatown, who demands payment from him if he does not want his cousin to be sold into bondage. He has to make sure to get her safely across the border before he can go look for his wife and son. Besides having learned to speak multiple languages (Chinese, English, and Spanish) by this point in his life, Bobby is clearly more of a transnational subject who is able to manage a situation with Chinese gangs, and he proves to be much more heroic than Emi precisely because he cares about his family. Thus Yamashita's novel offers an alternative to the oft-queered figure of the Asian male, and shows that the traditionally female-coded notions of the past and family life do not interfere with the heroism of a given character.

As another form of transnational illegal trade, the narrative strand revolving around Bobby's Rafaela touches on the transnational black market for organ transplants. The son of her neighbor at Gabriel's ranch, Doña Maria, whom she had heard was a middleman for importing and exporting "oranges from Brazil," turns out to be a black-market dealer of children's organs. Piecing together a conversation that she overhears at Doña Maria's house, Rafaela finds out that the content of a plastic cooler in her neighbor's refrigerator is a fresh baby's heart (118). The baby's heart is another register of traffic between the global South and the global North, reflecting a new division within the reorganized global economy. The anthropologist Nancy Scheper-Hughes calls this division a "medical apartheid" that has separated the world into two populations—organ givers and organ receivers: "The spirit of a triumphant global and 'democratic' capitalism' has released a voracious appetite for 'fresh' bodies from which organs can be procured. The confluence in the flows of immigrant workers and itinerant kidney sellers who fall prey to sophisticated but unscrupulous transnational organ brokers is a subtext in recent history of globalization."[50] Yamashita's novel gives literal form to Deleuze and Guattari's characterization of late capitalism "an organ-machine . . . plugged into an energy-source-machine,"[51] or pure reserves of organs and labor.

Back in East L.A., Buzzworm's narrative shows how U.S.-led global capitalism is equally responsible for the disenfranchisement of the underprivileged global migrants and racial minorities who share the space of the inner city. During the course of the novel, Buzzworm deals with two successive deaths of characters who live in the neighborhood. Although one is a black teenager and another is a Mexican street vendor, the deaths of these minor characters are remarkably similar. In both cases, their deaths are chalked up to drug overdose by the authorities despite evidence to the contrary. The black teenager dies from the urban violence of the gangs:

> He was beat up bad; hardly recognized the kid. Eyes were two big swollen purple bruises. Mouth and nose same thing. Head blows. Body blows. The whole anatomy all punched out. Kid had one of those thin builds with a fast metabolism on a sudden growth spurt. Now everything was swollen flesh. What are they talking about? Drugs. Coroner's saying he OD'd. Boy was beat to death. (104)

The Mexican street vendor, Margarita, who sold her fruit at a street corner that Buzzworm used to go to frequently, dies in a waiting room of the emergency room for lack of adequate medical attention:

> Mami! Mami! Wake up! Wake up! What's happened? They dragged her to emergency. It took hours to get in. The older kid knew when she was dead. He couldn't hear her heart, couldn't hear her breathe anymore. Sat there in the waiting room, holding her head, keeping the news to himself, scared to tell the younger ones, wanting to know what he was supposed to do, wanting to be young and stupid again. What he couldn't understand was what the folks at emergency were trying to tell him, trying to tell him it looked like his momma died of an overdose. Looked like she took too much. Too much of what? He wanted to know. Too much of work? (106–7)

But just as poignant is the old yard man at Gabriel's ranch, who lost his son because ambition and lack of opportunity in post-NAFTA Mexico had actually made him seek out organized crime:

> "Such a fool. Such a big shot. He used to carry a gun and fly a plane. He used to bring things: hard liquor, cigarettes, perfumes. I made him take it all away. It was a matter of time. They shot him in the head through the window of his car." (146)

While these deaths lie at the very margins of the novel and are given only a few lines or a paragraph, otherwise unmemorable and anonymous,

Yamashita manages to communicate the incalculable loss of each life for the grieving family member left behind.

Identifying the Imperial-Colonial Register in Monique Truong's *The Book of Salt* (2003)

Monique Truong's *The Book of Salt* (2003) is a novel that can't really exist. How can a story be told in English for us to understand in English, when its narrator does not speak English? A Vietnamese cook who finds himself in Paris during the 1920s and 1930s, the novel's first-person narrator Bình is a non-English speaker who only knows a few English phrases learned aboard the ship that took him from Vietnam to Paris: "please, thank you, hello, good-bye, beer, whiskey, rum, that-man-took-your-money, I-did-not-sleep-with-your-girl, I quit."[52] Although we are told that English still remains "a locked door" (150), Bình narrates his story in eloquent English, its parameters drawn by the kind of English that far exceeds practical use; it is the kind of English that Bình could never have shared with Stein's admirer and Bình's heartless lover Marcus Lattimore, who taught him of "their lush interiors, the secrets words can keep" (107) before disappearing from his life. By presenting us with a perspective from the margins, all the while indicating that this subjectivity *does not exist*, Truong's narrative resolves Gayatri Spivak's caveat that "the subaltern is necessarily the absolute limit of the place where history is narrativized into logic."[53]

None of this rhetorical structure has to register to the general reader; the seductive language in which the narrative is told provides enough of a smokescreen. The important thing is for Bình's story to reach across the global divide to be heard. If Habermas is right that a social bond is created through the illocutionary act of communication and not necessarily the locutionary content of what is being said, then the mere fact that Bình's story reaches an American audience may be all that is necessary. In fact, the less apparent it is that this is a mediated narrative, that it is really only with Truong that the reader is communicating, the better. In that regard, Truong's writing mimetically reproduces the labor of the global migrant, for whom remaining invisible is a crucial part of the servitude. The mask that Truong wears as Bình is well secured throughout, and only toward the end of the book, when we are told that Bình is not truly the narrator's name, is there a seemingly mystifying but potentially demystifying moment that reveals the narrative to be Truong's ventriloquism. Bình is not his name because the story belongs to countless other global migrants in servitude who are like Bình. At the same time, of course Bình is not the narrator's name; it is always Truong that we were listening to.

The locutionary content does matter, however. Stein and Toklas cannot perceive Bình's interiority, nor do they know that Bình already has a culinary mastery of French cuisine, having cultivated in Vietnam the ability to prepare French dishes with more skill and sophistication than her European and American characters could ever hope for. The readers can see the boldness with which Bình's narrative challenges the cultural authority of Stein and Toklas. At a moment when critical attention to U.S. literature and culture should continue to require heightening sensitivity to the "connective tissues binding America to the rest of the world," as Wai Chee Dimock has suggested,[54] Truong's narrative contextualizes an American cultural icon (Stein, with Toklas) within world history that includes French colonization of Vietnam, and takes language and food as parallel colonial-imperial registers of abjection and identification. Departing from Asian American writing that is bounded within the United States, Truong's narrative vision does away with the danger of unwittingly reinforcing a cultural tendency of U.S. exceptionalism by moving the story to Paris. Since both "immigrants" and "minorities" are notions that only make sense within a national framework, a singular focus on the flow of global migration into the United States is at the same time a premature dismissal of countless other forms of global traffic *from* the United States or an even greater number of global migrations *entirely outside of* the United States. In a narrative that grapples with anonymous and traditionally forgotten lives of Asian migrant laborers in Europe, shaped by legacies of Western imperialisms, Truong's novel brings U.S. history into conversation with a larger dynamic of global history in ways that these other primary texts do not.

A strong critical force that drives the novel is Truong's extraordinary ability to map out a continuum between an old imperial-colonial divide created by French imperialism and a newly emerging global divide, created by a deterritorialized form of late capital that is increasingly led by the United States. Truong's narrator and protagonist Bình grows up in Vietnam, spending much of his time working as a *garde-manger* in the kitchen of the French Governor-General's residence. In 1934, as the novel opens, Bình has been in Paris for eight years, the last five of which he has spent employed as a cook by fictional characters based on Gertrude Stein and Alice B. Toklas. Told in a dizzyingly nonlinear fashion with frequent jumps to the formative years of his childhood, the narrative switches back and forth between Saigon and Paris. The disorienting structure of the novel finds anchor in the spatial continuum laid out between various domestic spaces of the kitchen, which is the only consistent factor in Bình's life. The culinary skill he had obtained in Saigon had turned him into "a great commodity" in Paris, allowing him the freedom to "live like a migrating bird, a fish in a barrierless sea," which he describes as "a blessing that is also a curse" (189). Still, having gone through an "embarrassing number of households" in Paris before he finds steady employment with "the Steins," Bình seems to have accepted a life served out in the kitchen, "content to grow old in them, calling my stove my lover, calling the copper pans my children" (19).

In *The Book of Salt*, Vietnamese food is banished to the corner, even within Vietnam. No Vietnamese dishes are to be found in the kitchen of the Governor-General's house in Saigon, where Truong's narrator and protagonist Bình spends his younger days as a *garde-manger*. Under the "unflinching rallying cry" of Governor-General's wife commanding that everything should be done "As if in France!" (47), Bình grows up learning how to sculpt potatoes into perfect little spheres and carve chunks of turnips into swans (14). His older brother Anh Minh the Sous Chef, considered by his family to have made a successful life out of his career, believes that his own promotion to the first Vietnamese chef at the Governor-General's household depends upon the mastery of French language and culinary arts, and is intent on producing dishes with elegant French names that invoke imperial power at every turn—a perfect *omelette à la bourbonnaise, coupe ambassadrice,* or *crème marquise.*

Indochinese food materials and customs are in fact transformed into the very symbol of the abject created in the historical process of colonialism. In a hotel recognized as the most fashionable establishment in all of Indochina, the Continental Palace Hotel, a half-French, half-Vietnamese chef de cuisine is promptly dismissed for serving "dishes obscured by lemongrass and straw mushrooms," the guests outraged at the audacity of the "native cook" who dared "slip pieces of rambutan and jackfruit into the sorbets" (42). At the Governor-General's house, his wife is overheard expressing her absolute disdain of locals when she dictates a letter to her sister deriding the Vietnamese for using soymilk: "Imagine living among people who have tasted only a mother's milk![W]hat the Indochinese called 'milk' was only water poured over crushed dried soybeans!" (47). The Vietnamese servants come to recognize cow's milk as being explicitly an enabling symbol of the French, for when the new chef Blériot arrives from France, the chauffeur claims that it is "cow's milk in its immeasurable terms" that makes him a "remarkable specimen of French manhood" (59). Yet when milk introduced by the French to the Vietnamese begins to be produced locally, it immediately becomes suspect, as Madame begins to develop a distrust, if not fear and loathing, of local milk. Her reaction is based on rumors ranging from alleged filthiness specific to Indochina ("In this tropical heat," Madame had been told, "it is not unheard of for the milk to spoil as it is leaving the beast's sweaty udder") to an equally threatening idea that the anti-imperialist insurgency of Vietnamese has plotted to poison the milk ("The Nationalists have been feeding the cows here a weed so noxious that the milk, if consumed in sufficient amounts, would turn a perfectly healthy woman barren").

Of course, sweat glands in cows are mostly completely developed on the muzzle, so that perspiration that appears on its body is almost imperceptible in whatever tropics of Indochina the Governor-General's wife might be dreaming of. Nevertheless, she orders her chef to come up with a way of not using milk in making her favorite dishes. What is ironic is that while she thinks she has avoided the almost completely fabricated idea of "the beast's sweaty udder" altogether, that command produces a situation in which the sweat of the cooks will pour into the dish instead. On what was to be Bình's last night working at the Governor-General's house, his brother Anh Minh and the crew of his strongest men beat buckets of egg whites and shovels of white sugar in oversized copper bowls in order to make *oeufs à la neige* (eggs in snow) for the sixty-two guests invited by the Governor-General's wife for her birthday party. Instead of the *crème anglaise* that the original recipe requires, they are making *sabayon* sauce, created by whisking egg yolks with sugar and dry white wine over the lowest possible flame: "Sweat beads descended from necks, arms, and hands and collected in the bowls. Their salt, like the copper and the ice, would help the mixture take its shape" (46). This would be the real source of abjection for the Governor-General's wife, the servitude and labor of the locals involved, not the local materials procured for the French; the horror of local milk is a projection of the disavowed local labor that she cannot help but know.

Julia Kristeva identifies food loathing as the most elementary and most archaic form of abjection, experienced as a massive and sudden feeling of uncanniness: "familiar as it might have been in an opaque and forgotten life, [it] now harries me as radically separate, loathsome. . . . On the edge of nonexistence and hallucination, of a reality that, if I acknowledge it, annihilates me."[55] Kristeva in fact uses milk as an example of such revulsion:

> When the eyes see or lips touch that skin on the surface of milk—harmless, thin as a sheet of cigarette paper, pitiful as a nail paring—I experience a gagging sensation, and still farther down, spasms

> in the stomach, the belly. . . . Along with the sight-clouding dizziness, *nausea* makes me balk at that milk cream, separates me from the mother and father who proffer it. "I" want none of that element, sign of their desire; "I" do not want to listen, "I" do not assimilate it, "I" expel it. (3)

In Truong's work, when the Governor-General's wife uses cow's milk as delineation between herself and the colonized, she is immediately beset by the idea of the strangeness in cow's milk produced by the colonized rather than cow's milk produced back in "Mother France." Almost the same but not quite the same, cow's milk in Indochina becomes an embodiment of the *uncanny*, prompting a kind of horror particular to "what was once well known and had long been familiar" (in Freud's formulation).[56] The fantasy of milk spoiled by tropic heat and defiled by cow's sweat is a telling one that exposes her fear of that nightmare physically entering her body.

Abjection is thus tightly bound up with the process that goes into the construction of self. "It isn't the lack of cleanliness or health that causes abjection," Kristeva goes on to write, but "what disturbs identity, system, order" (4). The abject is "a jettisoned object" radically excluded and rejected as everything that is opposed to "I," which nevertheless will not cease to draw the subject "toward the place where meaning collapses." She explains that premeditated criminality is especially abject because it keenly exposes the fragility of judicial order. The Governor-General's wife is disgusted with the thought of milk defiled by cow's sweat, but it is significant that she might be more terrorized by the other rumor that the locals have poisoned cow's milk. The fantasy of the local's premeditated criminality here exposes the volatility of the exploitative system imposed by French imperialism that gives her power to oversee a household staff of fifteen locals. Like all other French wives of "government-clerk husbands," as Bình points out, the Governor-General's wife liked to forget who they really were, that they "had to cross oceans to move up a class" (44). "As if in France!" the Governor-General's wife may command, but Bình is quick to note that it requires her willful refusal to acknowledge the fact that "in France she would have only three instead of fifteen to serve her household needs" (46).

When the Governor-General's wife fears that the poisoned milk will cause barrenness in French women, she calls it "an unsolicited horror and bodily affront to Mother France" precisely because what she actually finds to be disturbing is that French rule over its colony will no longer be reproduced, that it is simply a system that can be overturned. If Kristeva thinks of abjection as something that will "not cease challenging its *master*" (2, emphasis mine) from the place of banishment, Truong's narrative coaxes this idea out of a metaphysical realm by literalizing this notion of the abject within the historical context of Western colonization in Vietnam.

The sixty-two guests invited by the wife of the French Governor-General for her birthday, festively poised to enjoy their *oeufs à la neige* is thus a powerfully loaded image:

> one hundred twenty-four turban-shaped islands of meringue, criss-crossed by fine lines of caramelized sugar bobbing around the crystal bowls brimming with the now chilled *sabayon* sauce

The perfectly innocent-looking white confectionary and the equally innocent language used to describe it both match exactly the occasion itself: A (literal) sugarcoating of an exploitative imperialist enterprise. This birthday party is at its core celebrating nothing other than the social reproduction of imperial rule. That the locally produced milk is replaced by eggs in the *sabayon* sauce is thus fitting for the occasion. Empire desires nothing more than to maintain the illusion that its pleasure is not predicated on the toiling colonial laborers (salt rendered imperceptible) while perfectly content to enjoy the benefits of colonial labor (sugar, the production of which colonialism reaps profit), and that involves celebrating another year in social reproduction ("Eggs in the Snow," made almost entirely of eggs). In Truong's vision, sugarcoated imperial fantasy experienced as pleasure and leisure is impossible without a willful *un*seeing that demands invisibility of any residues of labor.

The shape of Bình's servitude, once he arrives in Paris, remains almost exactly the same as it was in Saigon when it comes to being kept just as busy "with the culinary bustle that is the foundation of a continually entertaining household." Overtly imperialist abjection is no longer easy to place in Bình's life in France, but the structure of feeling remains the same. Sugar and eggs do continue to be associated with Bình's invisible servitude as the cook, signifiers of imperial desire for pleasure and reproduction of its social order. For Stein's guests at 27 rue de Fleurus stopping by for Saturday tea, Bình works in the kitchen creating nothing but desserts: "Rectangular folds of puff pastry dough, circles of *paté brisée*, bowls of heavy cream whipped with and without sugar, fresh fruit purées, fondant flowers and chocolate leaves, these are the basic components of sweetness that fill my days and someone else's mouth" (86). His hidden servitude is represented through another image of a dessert offered to the guests at Stein's Saturday teas: "My presence, just inside the entrance to my Mesdames' kitchen, ensures that all the cups are steaming and that the tea table stays covered with marzipan and butter-cream-frosted cakes. Always discreet, almost invisible, I imagine that when the guests look my way they see, well, they see a floor lamp or a footstool. I have become just that" (149). The image of Anh Minh's crew of strongest men laboring through the night overlaps with that of Bình standing in the kitchen of a sleeping household beating six eggs to make omelets: "While you have been waking up to the aroma of coffee brewing, dressing to the hushed rhythm of other people's labor, I have been in the kitchen since I was six and in your kitchen since six this morning. In my life as a minor domestic, a bit character in your daily dramas, I have prepared thousands of omelets" (154).

Here, the text suggests that the emerging global divide redrawn by a dynamic that will be fully articulated in late capitalism—in which the United States starts to play an increasingly leading role—is one in which exploitative structures are harder to detect than older forms of Western imperialism. Milk in France elicits only a visceral reaction of abjection, but this seems to have little to do with legible imperial fantasy. It is only when the milk is in stages of decay that it becomes abject, experienced as "the tang of soured milk" that the tongue cannot ignore (178). What is emphasized here is actually the absence of abjection in Gertrude Stein's affect. Stein claims that her olfactory senses are a "dismal failure," and Alice B. Toklas observes that Stein "would rather drink a glass of spoiled milk than bother to smell it beforehand" (181). Stein's inability to identify the abject goes so far as to shaping a part of who she is, as she claims that her inability to detect the varying stages of a patient's bodily decay was the root cause of her failure in medical school, which she had to drop out of to have come to Paris in the first place. The point seems to be that it is difficult to identify any of the sort of visible and intentional form of oppression and exploitation at 27 rue de Fleurus that we had seen at the Governor-General's household.

The submerged nature of Bình's narrative is also underscored by the fact that "*The Book of Salt*" happens to be the title of a fictional Gertrude Stein manuscript that appears in the novel. Desperate to capture the attention of his love interest Lattimore, an avid Stein admirer and frequenter of her salon, Bình tells him that he knows where the draft of her latest work is kept (19). Lattimore, in turn, is so enthralled with the idea of getting his hands on an unpublished Stein manuscript that he tries to talk Bình into taking it. Acutely aware of the risk he cannot afford to take, but ultimately unable to resist his entreaties, Bình finally relents. But when he flips through the pages of the manuscript before bringing it to Lattimore's apartment, Bình is able to recognize his name in an otherwise incomprehensible English text and realizes that Stein had been writing about him. Tracing his name that appears again and again at various points of the page, Bình is suddenly overwhelmed by the feeling that he is witnessing himself drowning, "surrounded on all sides by strangers, strung along a continuously unraveling line that keeps them above the water's surface" (214). Bình feels violated by Stein's sense of entitlement to narrate his own life and feels justified in the act of taking the manuscript, rationalizing that "the notebook may belong to my Madame, but the story, it belongs to me." The content of Stein's story about Bình can only be guessed by the fact that Lattimore abandons him after reading the manuscript, leaving behind only a note scribbled hastily in French: "Bee, thank you for *The Book of Salt*. Stein captured you, perfectly" (238).

The impossibility of Bình's narrative is crucial insofar as it allows Truong to get around the problematic nature of the subaltern who cannot speak. David Eng offers a nuanced analysis that *The Book of Salt* is "less an instance of the subaltern writing back than an exploration of the limits of such writing for the politics of history," as the narrative is constructed precisely in such a way as to make this impossibility itself to be visible.[57] Stein's writing, which would be circulated widely and internationally, will drown out the narratives belonging to someone like Bình, while the significance of her famous literary salon also easily obscures Bình's labor that serves its guests. Bình is a faint presence for the guests at the Steins', not a person but a utility: "Always discreet, almost invisible, I imagine that when the guests look my way they see, well, they see a floor lamp or a footstool. I have become just that" (149); if a fire was to strike 27 rue de Fleurus, Bình tells us, "Miss Toklas would run back into the burning apartment until every sheet of paper touched by GertrudeStein [*sic*] was safe in her arms" but "as for the cook, the assembled guests would scratch their heads and ask, 'The Steins have a cook?'" (150). Because his is a world that normally stays hidden, an untold story, there is a direct relationship between a lack of access to Western language and his place in the kitchen, which both serve as a shorthand for colonized space. Here, Truong's novel signals the manifestation of a new kind of U.S. imperialism that runs on an emerging culture industry and its global capital, now working together with the earlier form of French imperialism established in the nineteenth century. Stein and other U.S. émigrés are effectively on the same footing as the French, their wealth directly and indirectly drawn from a shared source of exploited labor in Indochina and other colonized spaces.

Bình's story is in fact not so unique; it is one that belongs to countless other bodies in global migration, whose collective itinerary has long been absent from Western historiography. His fate may be perceived as being interchangeable with stories belonging to the many seeking their way out of colonized spaces, only to be confined to the status of a silent migrant laborer once they reach the metropolis. In Paris, where the chimney pots framed by the open windows constitute "a landscape reserved for the very rich or the very poor," Bình experiences an acute sense of double-consciousness as he becomes aware of the loss of individuality: "Foreigner, *asiatique*, and, this being Mother France, I must be Indochinese. They do not care to discern any further, ignoring the question of whether I hail from Vietnam, Cambodia, or Laos. Indochina, indeed. We all belong to the same owner, the same Monsieur and Madame" (152). In Bình's own words: "I am but one within a long line of others. The Algerian orphaned by a famine, the Moroccan violated by his uncle, the Madagascan driven out of his village because his shriveled hand was a sign of his mother's misdeeds" (19). The stories might each be inflected by dramatically individual circumstances ranging from devastating natural disaster, violent family history, or unforgiving irrationality that dictate social structures everywhere. But their personal tragedies are nevertheless tightly bound up with each other, for their lives all take shape in the colonial spaces under French rule until after World War II.

Bình explicitly reminds us that his perceived inability to speak English should by no means reduce him to an inarticulate existence altogether: "fluency, after all, is relative. On that sheet of paper, on another side of the globe, I am fluent" (8). Case in point, Bình observes that Stein herself never gains complete mastery of French. From *The Autobiography of Alice B. Toklas*, sprinkled with Matisse and Picasso speaking in French and a description of Stein recommending that Toklas take French lessons, to Stein's essay *Paris France*, which opens with the remark that "I was only four years old when I was first in Paris and talked french [*sic*] there and was photographed there and went to school there" (1) and the statement that "French is a spoken language and English is really not" (5), one is used to assuming Stein's proficiency in French. I mention this only to highlight the fact that Stein never really wrote to a French audience and that her mythical status mostly registers to an English-speaking audience. Stein's limitedness in French is portrayed as a choice, "her habit never to master any language but her own": "Her French, like mine, has its limits. It denies her. It forces her to be short if not precise. In French, GertrudeStein finds herself wholly dependent on simple sentences." Bình is impressed by the way in which lack of access to French does not seem to affect Stein's self-confidence: "She compensates with the tone of her voice and the warmth of her eyes. She handles it with stunning grace. When I hear her speak it, I am filled with something very close to joy. I admire its roughness, its unapologetic swagger" (34). If Stein's transcendent aesthetic sensibility would never be called into question solely based on her French proficiency, by that very logic Bình's own limitations in English should not be read as signaling an innate lack of a sophisticated sensibility.

Toward the beginning of the novel, a bemused Gertrude Stein asks: "Thin Bin, how would *you* define 'love'"? Pointing to a table with ripening quinces in a blue and white china bowl, Bình shakes his head and leaves the room wordlessly. His silent response is far from an indication that Bình has no answer or lacks imagination, we find out shortly afterward, when he unravels the meaning of his gesture: "Quinces are ripe, GertrudeStein, when they are the yellow of canary wings in midflight. They are ripe when their scent teases you with the snap of green apples and the perfumed embraces of coral roses. But even then quinces remain a fruit, hard and obstinate—useless, GertrudeStein, until they are simmered, coddled for hours above a low, steady flame. Add honey and water and watch their dry, bone-colored flesh soak up the heat, coating itself in an opulent orange, not of the sunrises that you never see but of the insides of tree-ripened papayas, a color you can taste. To answer your question, GertrudeStein, love is not a bowl of quinces yellowing in a blue and white china bowl, seen but untouched." For Bình, "love" is not just a ripening of a fruit, but something that requires hours of labor. Words are also like quinces—hard and obstinate—useless, until the reader's attention simmers it, coddles it above the low, steady flame of our interest that readies us to consume the meaning of an ungraspable *Other.*

Chick Lit Goes to Wall Street: Min Jin Lee's *Free Food for Millionaires* (2007)

"Our crowns have been bought and paid for—all we have to do is wear them." Min Jin Lee's *Free Food for Millionaires* is prefaced by a James Baldwin quote from Toni Morrison's eulogy in the December 20, 1987, *New York Times,* "James Baldwin: His Voice Remembered; Life in His Language." In this eulogy, Morrison pays tribute to the way that Baldwin inhabited language, decolonizing "a forbidden territory" and opening up its use for African American writers: "[Baldwin] ungated it for black people so that in your wake we could enter it, occupy it, restructure it in order to accommodate our complicated passion . . . all the while refusing 'to be defined by a language that has never been able to recognize [us].'" The way he did so gave others courage to appropriate "an alien, hostile, all-white geography because [Baldwin] had discovered that 'this world is white no longer and it will never be white again.'" If Lee's best-selling novel can be read as an appropriation of a genre of popular fiction that normally features a young, single, white, and middle-class woman as its heroine, and if that appropriation can also be read as a social critique of the empty but oppressive structures of consumer-driven capitalism fueled by the forces of global finance, then the novel is a unique response to Baldwin's notion of the artist in a commercialized world *through* commercial fiction. In "Mass Culture and the Creative Artist," Baldwin wrote that the job for the creative artist is to ask "why the lives we lead on this continent are mainly so empty, so tame and so ugly," because without confronting this question, "we cannot possibly become what we would like to be."[58]

Nowhere else in *Free Food for Millionaires* is the resonance to Edith Wharton's *The House of Mirth* as noticeable as when the Korean American protagonist, Casey Han, tries her hand at hatmaking. A recent Princeton graduate struggling to make her living on her own in New York City during the 1990s, Casey is humbled by the fact that none of the skills she cultivated during college means much in the classes at FIT, where her crooked stitches earn her a C+ in "construction grade."[59] "So what was it that you'd studied at Princeton?" becomes a running joke with her more capable deskmates. In Wharton's novel, the former socialite Lily Bart's dizzying social descent takes her from the privileged spaces of the leisure class to Madame Regina's millinery seeking employment, which establishes that Lily has "joined the working classes."[60] The sharp rebuke Lily receives from the forewoman over *her* crooked stitches, "look at those spangles, Miss Bart,—every one of 'em sewed on crooked," accompanied one of the original illustrations by A. B. Wenzell that appeared in *Scribner's Magazine* in 1905.

Edith Wharton's readers openly expressed disappointment with the ending of *The House of Mirth* that followed the workroom scene at Madame Regina's: Lily is let go from the millinery only to wander around the streets in the cold and ultimately die in solitude from an overdose of sleeping drops. Although Wharton saw herself as a writer of serious fiction and disdained the popular novelist,[61] *The House of Mirth* was an extreme commercial success and captured a wide popular audience that included those she saw as being "better off [with the] innocuous dalliance with light literature."[62] For those readers, Amy Blair argues, "the novel's tragedy was not Lily's destruction itself but her inability to remain in the society in which she nearly had a foothold." These readers deliberately "misread" *The House of Mirth*, taking pleasure in consuming the novel's lush description of Lily's surroundings while turning a blind eye to Wharton's social critique itself: "identifying with Lily, [they] imaginatively read Lily's downfall as an injustice wrought by a cruel author rather than the inevitable outcome of an upwardly striving life." Thus the *Detroit Post* ran a story about a reader who accosted Wharton in the streets of Lenox, Massachusetts: "It was bad enough that you had the heart to kill Lily. But here you are, shamelessly parading the streets in a red hat!"[63] That the reader finds fault in Wharton "parading the streets in a red hat" is a particularly telling detail, since it's likely that a character in the novel itself, like Bertha Dorset, would feel no shame in "parading" her expensive Vionet hat in blue tulle, which in fact she does when she passes through Madame Regina's millinery for a touch-up at the height of Lily's misery in the back room of the millinery. Bertha is one of the characters largely to blame for sacrificing Lily's already frail social standing by publicly accusing her of stealing her husband in order to cover up her own affair, which creates a public scandal that brings about Lily's disinheritance. In the same sweeping gesture of cold-heartedness and self-protectionism, Bertha also drops her young protégé Ned Silverton with nothing but the debt that he incurred while living among the rich, which in turn devastates his sisters by wiping out their small fortune.

For the mass audience of popular fiction today, Casey's narrative unfolds in a way that is much more comforting, as one might expect from the differences in the hatmaking scenes. In Wharton's millinery workroom scene, Lily is told to hand the hat over to her peer Miss Kilroy after stripping the overlapping spangles that she had inadequately sewn onto the hat frame. As is the general tendency in the series of events in *The House of Mirth*, Lily is given no chance to redeem herself. By contrast, we see Casey on her third attempt at pick-stitching the belted ribbon into the gathered beret that is her homework assignment. Her hard work is not completely in vain, and she earns a B+ for her "design grade," receiving her millinery instructor's begrudging comment that she "see[s] improvement" (121). Where Lily feels tired and confused after the failure to sew the spangles on straight, wondering if her ineptitude was due to her growing distaste for her task or if she actually had some "physical disability," Casey is "humbled . . . but not in a bad way." Unlike Lily, once proud of her ability to trim her own hats but later disillusioned about her own lack of artistry in hatmaking, Casey still marvels at the way in which "a flat square of fabric become a baseball hat and a leftover piece of felt grow into a rosette" (121). Casey's venture into hatmaking happens early in the novel and is followed by a fairly standard progress narrative in which Casey moves on from the low-level administrative job at an investment bank and the weekend stint in retail sales toward a more ambitious career path in Wall Street. She goes on to apply (and is admitted) to business school at NYU, luckily gets into an internship program at the big investment banking firm Kearn Davis, and ends up making it into the top five of the candidates. She is given a chance to claim the one dream job that she had failed to get when she graduated from Princeton, displaying a kind of mastery over her destiny that is denied to Lily. Casey even has the power to reject the Wall Street job, deciding not to go back to business school to finish the degree. The novel ends with Casey dreaming about turning her hatmaking into a livelihood (559).

One obvious question that this ending leaves unanswered is how Casey would be able to pay back the large debt she accumulated during the four years since her graduation. In *The House of Mirth*, it is important that Lily pays back in full the debt owed to her friend's husband Gus Trenor, using all of her aunt's small legacy. Casey's credit-card debt is twenty-three thousand dollars by the end of the novel, the total sum of "the mounting clothing purchases and the humiliating cost of social life in Manhattan" (158), and she had also taken out loans to cover tuition for business school. To her ex-boyfriend Unu's remark that "it would be stupid to get into more debt if you don't get a degree," she replies only that "my life has become stupid" (559). The novel therefore ends with an escapist fantasy that everything will nevertheless be fine, closing with a happy vision of Casey and Unu intent on drawing a picture together on the sidewalk.

Heroines in the chick-lit genre are routinely ensnared in the kind of repetitive cycle of excessive consumption like Casey's, typically struggling with exorbitant credit-card bills that are somehow resolved in the end. Like Becky Bloomwood in the U.K. author Sophie Kinsella's Shopaholic series, Casey had not known how to balance her budget and amasses a debt of "twelve thousand dollars' worth of dinners out, flowers ordered, boxes of French chocolates, gym memberships, a pair of pearl earrings from Mikimoto, clothes and shoes, tuition for her hat classes" in no time (160); even when she has no means of paying back the debt anytime soon, not having the cash in her wallet or bank account doesn't "keep her from charging another round of drinks when she went out with the millinery girls or friends from school" (165); she finds herself in "a perennial state of buyer's remorse" (335). Chick-lit heroines do not usually suffer in the end from their romantic consumption, however, as they also belong to a world of formulaic fiction that remains fundamentally escapist, in John

Cawelti's classic formulation, "where conflicts are resolved and inescapable tensions and frustrations are temporarily transcended."[64]

Like a prototypical chick-lit heroine, Casey is particularly addicted to the fleeting moment of gratification in which an idealized self-image is imagined to be attained through shopping.[65] Her conspicuous consumption is an expression of ethnic/class anxiety, for as Casey snaps to her college friend Virginia when teased about the fuss she makes: "well, gee, honey, but you never get confused for a Japanese tourist, nanny, mail-order bride, or nail salon girl when you walk into a store, do you? What the hell do you know about it?" (69). But having a white-collar job in Wall Street doesn't resolve her anxiety about cultural belonging. The reason that Casey buys an outfit that "cost a breathtaking eleven hundred dollars—more than half her monthly take-home pay" (a purchase that "she could have passed on") (219) is that it makes her feel "legitimate in her shifting environments": "tonight, in this dress, she was a girl who'd gone to Andover, not Stuyvesant, and a girl who'd lost her virginity at the Gold and Silver in New York, not at a roller rink in Elmhurst."

When Casey's mentor figure Sabine Gottesman sees her caught in an addictive pattern of self-destructive consumption and overspending with no plans to change her life, she tells her that "all this spending is a substitute for what you really want. All this overspending is merely addiction" (169). But Sabine may not have gotten the entire picture. In Pamela Thoma's analysis, chick lit is an updated and revised version of romance fiction, in which heroines look to professional careers rather than romantic relationships for respect, reward, and recognition: "Romantic relationships in these novels are displaced by the neoliberal romance with the romance with the laboring self."[66] But it is that search for meaningful work in the neoliberal marketplace that is inextricably intertwined with conspicuous consumption: "production and consumption are intertwined, and 'good' citizens must continually cultivate and reinvent the self through acquiring and demonstrating that most important market qualification: marketplace expertise."[67] So although Sabine is well-meaning in goading Casey to apply for business school so she can raise her profile for a higher income, Wall Street may not be the best place to provide an answer for Casey's problems.

In Karen Ho's ethnography of Wall Street, *Liquidated*, the financial sector is revealed to be "[more of] an austere white-collar factory than the popularly imagined series of luxurious (but intense) power meetings and lunches in gleaming, high-tech surroundings," where demanding labor amounts to a contradiction between high aspiration and ambition on the one hand and mundane reality on the other (92). In *Free Food for*

Millionaires, the trading floor is described as "a white-collar assembly line with Aeron chairs," and although the floor where the investment bankers have their offices resembles "a private English men's club—mahogany paneling, silver-leaf-framed black-and-white photographs of New York's first skyscrapers, and buttoned leather chairs," this image takes on a prison-like cast with the large shared office for the junior analysts—the lowest rung in the front-office hierarchy—in which twenty Ivy grads were "chained to their rolltop desks" (78). Given this work environment, which can only sustain a fragile sense of raison d'être, Wall Streeters need affirmation of their exceptional status on a daily basis, leading to the justification of global market dominance and exploitation based on qualities that are encouraged in them, such as "intense hard work, motivation, exposure to greatness, risk-taking, and entrepreneurial resourcefulness": "Smartness leads to market dominance, not only because of explicit assumptions about talent and credibility but also through the premise that smartness is spatial, that it should rightly spread, colonize, and necessarily manifest as the natural determinant and arbiter of global market leadership" (69).

Deception, betrayal, and moral corruption are associated with Wall Street from the beginning of the novel, when Casey walks in on her college boyfriend Jay having a threesome with sorority girls from Louisiana State University whom he had brought home from a bar he had gone to with his investment banking colleagues after closing a deal. Later in the novel when Casey is doing her internship program at the same firm, Kearn Davis, she becomes involved with a colleague who invites her on a golf trip with clients, jeopardizing the relationship with her new boyfriend, Unu. Realizing that she had "done to Unu what Jay had done to her" in not considering his feelings, Casey feels that she went beyond her moral boundaries: "She had violated her own morality, however broken and taped up it might have been" (458). Unu himself is a Wall Street analyst who does maintain his moral integrity, but he is also driven to an excessive gambling addiction that ends up costing him his beloved car, a watch his father got him for graduation, and his apartment. Unu's gambling is a self-destructive reaction to the pressure from managing directors who are not happy with his refusal to gamble on his clients' money. As an analyst who believes in making recommendations for long-term profit investments based on solid research, Unu is behind the times in avoiding the kind of "reasonable" stock calls that maximize short-term profit: "Everything I like is a long shot, it turns out. But I did the research and I know what's good, it's just that the market is filled with a bunch of fucking hedgers. No one believes in companies anymore or wants to hold 'em up. Flip, flip, flip. That's all they do" (301).

A progress narrative in Wall Street, then, is also a narrative about loss of innocence and compromised integrity. This is a point that is most thoroughly portrayed through another Korean American character, Ted Kim, who introduces Casey to Wall Street. Ted came from a family of immigrant cannery workers, "anxious and hungry, running from Alaska" (53). Having built up a strong enough profile at an investment bank in the four years since his graduation from Harvard, Ted attends Harvard Business School as a Baker Scholar, and at the beginning of the novel he is an executive director at Kearn Davis slated to become a managing director in the upcoming year. In the novel, one of Ted's happiest moments is when his bid for a townhouse on East Seventieth is accepted for "just north of a million dollars" (173), which is "as big a deal as when he'd made managing director the year before—the youngest in the history of Kearn Davis." This immediately turns into a moment of intense disappointment, when his wife, Casey's friend Ella, doesn't join him in his excitement. Ted is unable to understand that their two-bedroom Upper East Side apartment might mean something to Ella, because it was purchased for them by her father. He also doesn't operate on the notion of an apartment being "enough" for them. He attributes Ella's silent reaction to a general lack of passion, which he then uses to justify his ongoing affair with the office assistant Delia. Ted's unfaithfulness is cast as a part of the corruption of values that attended his entry into Wall Street, prompted by his rejection of his working-class roots. When Ella finds out about Delia, Ted reflects on the way in which his family's poverty had made him so ashamed that he had thrown away the rare moral integrity that defined his parents' lives:

> He thought of church and God and all the things he had learned from his simple parents, about never lying or stealing or wanting something that you had no right to have, to know his place in the world and to never overreach, and how he had disagreed with so many of their tenets because he didn't want to be them. But now he thought: They never hurt me. Except by their failure. Ted clutched his head with both hands. The older men at the cannery always said that his father, Johnny Kim, was a man whose yes was yes and whose no was no. (187)

Although Wall Street itself only appears very briefly in *The House of Mirth,* the vacuous lives of the entire social circle of New York's elites are implicitly anchored to the activity and logic of the stock market. Lily Bart's spectacular social downfall is sharply defined against the upward mobility of the Jewish businessman Simon Rosedale, which is also influenced by the stock market. At the beginning of the novel, Rosedale is so desperate to break into Lily's social set that the idea of merely escorting her to Central Station as she headed off to stay in Bellomont, her wealthy friends' estate in Rhinebeck, appears as "money in his pocket" (16). By the end of the novel, when Lily has been all but ostracized from that set, Rosedale is in a position to restore Lily's social standing: "if you'd only let me, I'd set you up over them all—I'd put you where you could wipe your feet on 'em!" (326). Despite the kindness that Rosedale shows her when her former friends have disappeared from her life, Lily is struck by how much Rosedale's words reflect his "old standard of values," which she had rejected repeatedly, marked by a relentless pursuit for money, power, and elite status.

One might locate the beginning of Lily's troubles with her acceptance of the offer from her friend Judy Trenor's husband Gus to speculate for her in the stock market. Later, she finds out that the money he had given her had not come from the stock market but from his own bank account, and realizes to her horror that he expected her to "pay up" with "interest on one's money." Precisely around the time that Lily's reputation first becomes unstable because of the rumored ties to Gus Trenor, Rosedale gains a foothold into that same social set by having made an extremely lucrative speculation in the stock market, "placing Wall Street under the obligation which only Fifth Avenue could repay" (240). While Trenor's claim to having made money for Lily on the stock market was an outright lie, Rosedale had actually doubled his equity through his understanding of the global market:

> It had been a bad autumn in Wall Street, where prices fell in accordance with that peculiar law which proves railway stocks and bales of cotton to be more sensitive to the allotment of executive power than many estimable citizens trained to all the advantages of self-government. Even fortunes supposed to be independent of the market either betrayed a secret dependence on it, or suffered from a sympathetic affection: fashion sulked in its country houses, or came to town incognito, general entertainments were discountenanced, and informality and short dinners became a fashion. . . . The mere fact of growing richer at a time when most people's investments are shrinking, is calculated to attract envious attention; and according to Wall Street rumours, Welly Bry and Rosedale had found the secret of performing this miracle. (131–32)

The depreciation of railroad stocks corresponds to the actual state of the stock market in Wall Street during the early 1890s, as does the reduced output in "the bales of cotton." In 1890, as the collapse of the Argentine securities boom first dealt a blow to the British financial markets, leading railway securities at the New York Stock Exchange had already started to decline sharply as London investors withdrew speculative funds from American enterprises (estimated at the time to have been at least $500 million).[68] This eventually led to the Panic of 1893, a depression characterized by the failure of major railroads including Reading, Atchson, Erie, Union Pacific, and North Pacific. For instance, Union Pacific in 1893 sold for four dollars a share, although it had been previously assessed at fifteen dollars.[69] At the beginning of 1893, most American investors were reported to have been optimistic. But in Rosedale, Wharton created a character whose "London clothes" and business trips abroad indicate the international reach of his business, someone who might have been able to foresee the imminent crash and to bet against the market.

In *The House of Mirth,* the social progressives' attempts to curb the unprecedented levels of corporate power wielded by the railroad consolidation, of which Lily Bart's Fifth Avenue set would have been the primary beneficiaries, is portrayed as being successful. Wharton's narrator cites "a peculiar law" as another determining reason for the "bad autumn in Wall Street," suggesting that progressive government regulation ("the allotment of executive power") has infringed on monopoly capitalism, interfering with a market that until then had been "self-regulated" by "estimable citizens." The decrease of "bales of cotton" can be a general reflection of economic recession, but it can also be read as the result of government regulation that put an end to discriminatory practices of the railroad monopoly. Although historians dispute the effectiveness of the legislation, the 1887 Act to Regulate Commerce did establish the Interstate Commerce Commission (ICC) in order to confront the problem of "informational asymmetry between investors and managers in America's first big business, the railroads" and to regulate "rates, particularly to eliminate rate discrimination."[70] With the 1906 Hepburn Act, the ICC gained authority to set maximum rates on the railroad for the first time.[71]

Thus *The House of Mirth* aligns itself with concerns of Wharton's contemporary writers at the turn of the century, for whom the monopolistic practices of big corporations and corruption of the church, the press, or the government were a major issue.[72] Frank Norris's dramatization in *The Octopus* (1901) portrayed the railroad corporations as impersonal machinery that could gobble up fortunes and destroy the lives of one group of people while it enriched others. Around the time that the ICC was formed, Stewart Denison was also making an impassioned plea in *An Iron Crown: A Tale of the Great Republic* (1885):

> When four or five railway kings can steal one hundred and sixty millions in twenty years; when an oil company can pile fabulous millions on millions in ten years; when a Wall-street pirate can steal from the American people one hundred millions in twenty years by wrecking railroads, seizing telegraphs, and endangering the business interests of the countrywhen the rich grow enormously rich, and the poor daily poorer; when all these things can occur, under sanction of the law, in a great republic, is it not time to stop and think?[73]

Invoking canonical female writers of the Western literary tradition is a standard chick-lit convention, which can be seen in representative works of chick lit such as Helen Fielding's *Bridget Jones's Diary* (Jane Austen), Emma McLaughlin's *Nanny Diaries* (Charlotte Brontë), and Candice Bushnell's *Trading Up* (Edith Wharton).[74] This is consistent with the way in which Lee's novel generally embraces affective forms of reading practices that shape the experiences of a mass audience. For instance, the novel positively portrays Casey's naming of her hats after the images of her "favorite book women," collapsing the distinctions between writers and heroines ("Charlotte, Becky, Valerie, Lily, Edith, Jane, Anna, and Hazel" [554]). In Casey, Lee explicitly creates a heroine whose reading practice has not been trained in an academic setting. Casey was an economics major and was only familiar with "about twenty Penguin classics [read] on her own without any real instruction as to how to read them." She feels inhibited in discussing literary works with her classmates from Princeton, who had gone to private schools and majored in comp lit and English, whom she admired for "how confident they were about their likes and dislikes," coveting their "authority and ease with literature" (383). The level of confidence the Princeton friends display reflects an elite status that sets Casey apart from them. Even Casey's best friend in college, Virginia Craft, had read everything including Dante in Italian and all those volumes of Proust in French, and goes away to Italy for a master's degree in fine arts after graduation. Casey feels a divide rising between them "like a drawbridge sealing up a castle": "From the other side of the moat, Casey had to make her own way" (59).

Academic training in literature can be used for self-advancement, as in the case of Casey's college/Wall Street–bound boyfriend Jay. As an English major who wrote his senior thesis on Ovid's influence on Shakespeare, Jay lays claim to having carefully read more than twenty of Shakespeare's plays and most of his sonnets (133). Invited to a dinner with Casey at Sabine's house, Jay discusses the plot of *King Lear*, which had been playing at Lincoln Center, "pleased to exploit his English major for some useful purpose," and is ready to "recite sonnets after coffee." His ability to mirror Sabine's reaction to the tragic ending of the play with a "wide-eyed expression" works to his favor, and Jay's passion for the play impresses Sabine's husband, Isaac Gottesman. Isaac is a trustee at Columbia Business School, where Jay is wait-listed, and he walks out that evening with a pending call that would secure another interview with them that leads to his acceptance in their program. Unfortunately, Jay's familiarity with *King Lear* does not translate into any real form of empathy, and he lacks the ability to understand the complicated relationship Casey has with her father: "What was more troubling was . . . how he had never really understood what it was like to be her. It wasn't that a white person couldn't comprehend what it was like to be in her skin, but Jay, in his unyielding American optimism, refused to see that she came from a culture where good intentions and clear talk wouldn't cover all wounds. It didn't work that way with her parents, anyway. They were brokenhearted Koreans—that wasn't Jay's fault, but how was he supposed to understand their kind of anguish?" (153)

Casey's *amateur* love of literature is mostly kept private, but it brings about an unexpected friendship with an old man who owns a rare bookshop on Madison Avenue that she walks into one day, located across from the bus stop that she uses on her daily commute to work. The shopkeeper, Joseph McReed, tells her that he had often seen her carrying around novels by Thackeray, Hardy, and Eliot, among others. Emboldened by Joseph's assertion that "no doubt there must be many Korean Daisys or Beatrices or Juliets" (336), Casey engages in a conversation about *Middlemarch*:

> Feeling brave all of a sudden, she said, "Isn't Dorothea Brooke such a fool?"—denouncing Eliot's main character, whom Casey loved and disliked at the same time.
>
> "Yes. Principled individuals often are," he said. "But Eliot lets her have it. Dorothea marries old Casaubon. Now he's the fool! I feel quite sorry for Dorothea. She's just a young girl who believes too much," he said. Dorothea's husband, Casaubon, was a pedagogue who'd spent his life researching a big book that no one would ever read.
>
> "Yes, but Casaubon has his tragedy, too," she replied. "He had money and work, but not true love. You can't live without that," she blurted out.
>
> "No, you can't." Joseph nodded in sympathy.

> The book dealer looked hurt, and the sadness in his eyes made him look even older. What she'd said had upset him. Casey wished that she could afford to buy something. (340)

From the narrator's explanation of who Casaubon was, it is clear that the reader of *Free Food for Millionaires* is not expected to have read *Middlemarch*. It is the scholarly reader who is mocked via Casaubon as "a fool" for being "the pedagogue who'd spent his life researching a big book that no one would ever read" and had "no true love." What can be dismissed as the naïveté of Dorothea Brooke, Casey, and any reader who identifies herself as "a girl who believes too much," is subsequently embraced by the narrator.

This does not mean that Lee's novel encourages readers to abandon critical engagement. The dialogue is followed by Casey's decision to buy the first edition of *Jane Eyre* from the rare book shopkeeper, which serves as a commentary about the consumer-driven economy that dictates her life. The value of the rare book is not driven by the forces of neoliberal capitalism, and Casey's desire to "buy something" also has to do with wanting to respond to Joseph's pain. Casey stops to reflect on why she might not buy a rare book if she could spend a couple of hundred dollars on shoes. The purchase of the expensive *Jane Eyre* volume is the first instance in which Casey isn't charging the credit card to fill a void forever created by the dream object of consumer culture. Although Casey does not actually have the $1,500 to pay for the book, she ends up handing over her credit card to Joseph. Recognizing the difference between this purchase and her other shopping sprees, in which the persistent desire to attain the impossible ideal that capitalism promises but never delivers, Casey bravely tells Joseph that she is "better off" for having blocked off that amount of credit. Later, when she thinks of returning the book, she recalls the special moment when "Joseph had walked over to the shelf to pick out that book for her" (342), and finds that she treasured that memory. As Walter Benjamin writes in *Illuminations*, the collector is a quixotic figure, refusing to be swept away by the forces of modernity, which are ever driven toward the future:

> Every passion borders on the chaotic, but the book collector's passion borders on the chaos of memories. More than that: the chance, the fate, that suffuse the past before my eyes are conspicuously present in the accustomed confusion of these books. . . . [The collector's] existence is tiedto a relationship to objects which does not emphasize their functional, utilitarian value—that is their

> usefulness—but studies and loves them as the scene, the stage, of their fate.[75]

Book collecting actually appears at the very beginning of *The House of Mirth,* invoked as an antithesis to Lily Bart's buying of clothing. The young lawyer Lawrence Selden tells Lily that he likes to have "good editions of the books I am fond of" (11), and agrees with Lily that he wishes he was rich enough to buy all the books he wants. Selden's book collecting is distinguished from the preoccupation of collecting rare books that "fetch fabulous prices," exemplified by the wealthy Percy Gryce and his father's collection of Americana that is considered to be "the finest in the world." "Now and then I pick up something in the rubbish heap," Selden admits, saving from the ashes the volume that is otherwise deemed to be worthless. Lily sees Selden's book collecting as a luxury she can't afford, for her funds are tied up with the buying of fashionable clothing: "Your coat's a little shabby—but who cares? It doesn't keep people from asking you to dine. If I were shabby no one would have me: a woman is asked out as much for her clothes as for herself. The clothes are the background, the frame, if you like: they don't make success, but they are a part of it. Who wants a dingy woman? We are expected to be pretty and well-dressed till we drop—" (12). This worldview had been shaped by her late mother, who had taught Lily to disdain "people who 'lived like pigs'" (37). Although for the most part Lee's novel utilizes existing conventions of popular fiction, *Free Food for Millionaires* destabilizes the idea that preconceived notions that are handed down must be uncritically accepted. In one of the most important moments of the novel, Casey thinks about a Princeton classmate named John Pringle, whose family background would have allowed him to do anything he wanted. But he lacks imagination and believes he had no choice in life but to take up his family business, "toadying" after his father. The conclusion Casey draws is that "what mattered was not what you could do, but what you believed you could do" (383).

Notes

Introduction

1. John K. Young, *Black Writers, White Publishers: Marketplace Politics in Twentieth-Century African American Literature* (Jackson: University of Mississippi Press, 2006), 6.

2. Pierre Bourdieu, *The Field of Cultural Production: Essays on Art and Literature* (New York: Columbia University Press, 1993), 40; hereafter cited parenthetically. Bourdieu delineates two principles of hierarchization represented in the dichotomy between "bourgeois art" and "art for art's sake," the mainstream domain that is favorable to "those who dominate the field economically and politically" (heteronomous principle) and another domain in which advocates align themselves to "degree of independence from the economy, seeing temporal failure as a sign of election and success as a sign of compromise."

3. Henry Louis Gates Jr., *The Signifying Monkey: A Theory of African-American Literary Criticism* (New York: Oxford University Press, 1988), 49; hereafter cited parenthetically.

4. "The critic of comparative black literature also dwells at a sort of cross-roads, a discursive crossroads at which two languages meet, be these languages Yoruba and English, or Spanish and French, or even (perhaps especially) the black vernacular and standard English" (ibid., 65).

5. Evelyn Nien-Ming Ch'ien, *Weird English* (Cambridge: Harvard University Press, 2004), 11; hereafter cited parenthetically.

6. Michel de Certeau, *The Practice of Everyday Life*, trans. Steven Rendall (Berkeley: University of California Press, 1984), viii.

7. In Bourdieu's more general theorizing of the field of cultural production, "newcomers" adopt a similar practice: "repeating and reproducing [culture] in a sociologically non-congruent contexthas the effect of rendering it non-congruous or even absurd, simply by making it perceptible as the arbitrary convention that it is" (31).

8. Cyrus R. K. Patel, *Emergent U.S. Literatures: From Multiculturalism to Cosmopolitanism in the Late Twentieth Century* (New York: New York University Press,

2014). Patel goes on to add that the Native American writer Gerald Vizenor draws attention to "the parallels between native American and Chinese trickster traditions in his novel published that same year, *Griever: An American Monkey King in China* (33).

9. Gates, *Signifying Monkey*, 23. "In the jazz tradition, compositions by Count Basie ("Signify") and Oscar Peterson ("Signifying") are structured around the idea of formal revision and implication. When a musician 'signifies' a beat, he is playing the upbeat into the downbeat of the chorus, implying their formal relationship by merging the two structures together to create an ellipsis of the downbeat. The downbeat, then, is rendered present by its absence. This is a revision of an aspect of the blues. When playing the blues, a great musician often tries to make musical phrases that are elastic in their formal properties. These elastic phrases stretch the form rather than articulate the form. Because the form is self-evident to the musician, both he and his well-trained audience are playing and listening with expectation. Signifyin(g) disappoints these expectations; caesuras, or breaks, achieve the same function. This form of disappointment creates a dialogue between what the listener expects and what the artist plays."

10. King-Kok Cheung, *Articulate Silences: Hisaye Yamamoto, Maxine Hong Kingston, Joy Kogawa* (Ithaca: Cornell University Press, 1993), 4.

11. Bertolt Brecht, "Popularity and Realism," in Ernst Bloch, Georg Lukacs, Bertolt Brecht, and Walter Benjamin, *Aesthetics and Politics* (New York: Verso, 1980), 82.

12. Examples of actual events include the Benefit Reading for the United Farm Workers hosted by City Lights on February 26, 1972; and the Allende Neruda Memorial Reading at Glide Church on October 3, 1973.

13. Stephen Vincent to Rei Magosaki, e-mail, October 11, 2014: "I was the California State Coordinator for the Poetry in the Schools Program—with its offices at State. It was the job that enabled me to hire poets for workshops from diverse communities. Several of whom I went on to publish with either or both Shocks and Momo's Press. That job went for 2 years–1971–73."

14. Kenneth W. Warren, "The End(s) of African-American Studies," *American Literary History* 12, no. 3 (2000): 640.

15. I refer here to the work coauthored by Michael Hardt and Antonio Negri, *Empire* (Cambridge: Harvard University Press, 2001).

16. Trinh T. Minh-ha, *Woman, Native Other: Writing Postcoloniality and Feminism* (Bloomington: Indiana University Press, 1989), 7.

17. Sarah Brouillette, *Postcolonial Writers in the Global Literary Marketplace* (Houndmills: Palgrave Macmillan, 2007), 4; hereafter cited parenthetically.

18. Rachel Lee, "Asian American Cultural Production in Asian-Pacific Perspective," *boundary 2* 26, no. 2 (Summer 1999): 231–54.

19. David L. Eng, "The Ends of Race," in "Comparative Racialization," special issue, *PMLA* 123, no. 5 (October 2008): 1482–83.

20. Saskia Sassen, "The Logic of Finance: Abuse of Power and System Crisis," in *How They Got Away with It: White Collar Criminals and the Financial Meltdown*, ed. Susan Will, Stephen Hendelman, and David C. Brotherton (New York: Columbia University Press, 2013), 2.

21. Fon W. Boardman Jr., "Books Become Big Business: Wall Street Discovers Publishing," *Challenge*, March 1961; Boris Kachka, "The End," *New York Magazine*, September 14, 2008. By the 1990s, it was readily apparent to cultural critics that five big

transnational conglomerates were dominating the publishing industry. See Herbert C. Rudman, "Corporate Mergers in the Publishing Industry: Helpful or Intrusive?," *Educational Researcher* 19, no. 1 (January–February 1990): 14–20.

22. According to Suzanne Ferriss and Mallory Young's introduction to *Chick Lit: The New Woman's Fiction* (New York: Routledge, 2006), chick-lit books earned more than $71 million in 2002, prompting the establishing of separate imprints dedicated to the genre at presses like Harlequin, Broadway, and Pocket Books.

23. Brouillette is referring to Brennan's Salman Rushdie (36–37). Though Brouillette discredits this view, Graham Huggan's earlier and pioneering materialist assessment of postcolonial field of production stressed the role of the exotic in the commodification of postcolonial writing, in accommodating a particular kind of commodity fetishism that operates through "mystification (or leveling-out) of historical experience; imagined access to the cultural other through the process of consumption; [and] reification of people and places into exchangeable aesthetic objects" (Huggan, *The Postcolonial Exotic: Marketing the Margins* [New York: Routledge, 2001], 19).

24. Ned Stuckey-French, "'No Name Woman' by Maxine Hong Kingston," June 24, 2011, http://nedstuckeyfrench.com/essays-in-america/%E2%80%9Cno-name-woman%E2%80%9D-by-maxine-hong-kingston/.

25. Susan Koshy, "Minority Cosmopolitanism," *PMLA* 126, no. 3 (May 2011): 594.

26. Judith Butler, *Bodies That Matter: On the Discursive Limits of "Sex"* (New York: Routledge, 1993), referenced in Diana Fuss, *Identification Papers* (New York: Routledge, 1995), 11.

27. Pheng Cheah, *Inhuman Conditions: On Cosmopolitanism and Human Rights* (Cambridge: Harvard University Press, 2006).

28. Rita Felski, *Uses of Literature* (Malden, MA: Blackwell, 2008).

29. Kwame Anthony Appiah, *Cosmopolitanism: Ethics in a World of Strangers* (New York: Norton, 2006), 31.

30. Jonathan Weisman, "Deal Reached on Fast-Track Authority for Obama on Trade Accord," *New York Times*, April 16, 2015.

31. Joseph Stiglitz, "On the Wrong Side of Globalization," *New York Times*, March 15, 2014.

32. *Globe and Mail*, July 15, 2013.

1 / Trickster Poetics at the Turn of the Twentieth Century

1. At least fifty-one reported incidents occurred between 1855 and 1907. Major incidents: Rogue River, Oregon (1855), Salmon le Sac/Roslyn, Washington (1880), Tacoma, Washington (1885), Eureka, California (1885), Rock Springs, Wyoming (1885), Truckee, California, and Deep Creek and Snake River, Oregon (1887).

2. Ronald A. T. Judy, *(Dis)forming the American Canon: African-Arabic Slave Narratives and the Vernacular* (Minneapolis: University of Minnesota Press, 1993), 63; hereafter cited parenthetically.

3. Judy traces this rhetorical violence back to the conflation of whiteness and claim to intelligence in Kant's *Observations on the Feelings of the Beautiful and the Sublime* (1764). A highly questionable premise is revealed in Kant's writing when, in response to a black carpenter's "haughty" comment that "you whites are indeed fools, for first you make great concessions to your wives, and afterward you complain when they drive you mad," Kant states that "in short, this fellow was quite black from head to foot, a clear proof that what he said was stupid." Here, Judy questions the reasoning

of "the sign of blackness as negation, and the arbitrary relation between the speaking subject and his common humanity with the European" (106).

4. Charles Chestnutt, *The Conjure Woman* (1899; rpt., Ann Arbor: University of Michigan Press, 1969), 22; hereafter cited parenthetically.

5. Walter A. Plecker, who drafted the Racial Integrity Act of 1924, refers to a comb that hangs in a local church to determine the racial identity of a mixed-race applicant registering for birth and marriage records kept in Virginia from 1853 to 1896 ("If it passes through the hair of an applicant he is an Indian, if not, he is a negro") (Walter A. Plecker to Harry E. Davis, October 4, 1924, folder i, box 56, John Powell Papers, University of Virginia). This is mentioned in J. Douglas Smith's *Managing White Supremacy: Race, Politics, and Citizenship in Central Virginia* (Chapel Hill: University of North Carolina Press, 2002), chap. 3, n. 49.

Also, in Langston Hughes's *The Big Sea: An Autobiography* (1940; rpt., New York: Hill and Wang, 1993), a joke turns on the comb (103):

> "You black," said thc Kru man.
>
> "I can part my hair," said George, "and it ain't nappy."
>
> But to tell the truth, George shaved a part in his hair every other week, since the comb wouldn't work. The Kru man knew this, so they both laughed loudly, for George's face was as African as Africa.

6. Helen Bradley Foster, in *"New Raiments of Self": African American Clothing in the Antebellum South* (London: Bloomsbury, 1997), alludes to the following account from slave narratives collected in the mid-1930s as a part of the Federal Writers' Project: "Lucy Key (70 plus years): I recollect what we called after the War a 'Jim Crow.' It was a hairbrush that had brass or steel teeth like pins 'ceptin' it was blunt. It was that long, handle and all (about a foot long). They'd wash us and grease my legs with lard, keep them from looking ashy and rusty. Then they'd come after me with them old brushes and brush my hair. It mostly took skin, hair, and all (9.4: 198–99 [MS/AR], Library of Congress)," www.bergfashionlibrary.com/view/NEWRAIM/chapter-NEWRAIM0008.xml.

7. Eric Sundquist, *To Wake the Nations* (Cambridge: Harvard University Press, 1993), 275.

8. Sterling A. Brown, "Athletics and the Arts" (1951), in *A Son's Return: Selected Essays of Sterling A. Brown*, ed. Mark A. Sanders (Boston: Northeastern University Press, 1996), 126.

9. William Dean Howells, "Mr. Chesnutt's Stories," *Atlantic Monthly* 85 (May 1900): 700.

10. *Atlantic Monthly*, August 1898, qtd. by McElrath and Leitz in *"To Be an Author": Letters of Charles Chesnutt 1889–1905*, ed. Joseph R. McElrath Jr. and Robert C. Leitz III (Princeton, NJ: Princeton University Press, 1997), 110.

11. Chesnutt to Albion W. Tourgée, September 26, 1889, in *"To Be an Author,"* 45.

12. Chesnutt to Houghton, Mifflin, & Co., September 8, 1891, in *"To Be an Author,"* 75.

13. Robert C. Nowatzki, "'Passing' in a White Genre: Charles Chesnutt's Negotiations of the Plantation Tradition in 'The Conjure Woman,'" *American Literary Realism, 1870–1910* 27, no. 2 (Winter 1995): 24.

14. For an analysis that links the statistics of lynchings to the changing economy in the South, see E. M. Beck and Stewart E. Tolnay, "The Killing Fields of the Deep South: The Market for Cotton and the Lynching of Blacks, 1882–1930," *American Sociological Review* 55, no. 4 (August 1990): 526–39.

15. Peter Wallenstein, "Reconstruction, Segregation, and Miscegenation: Interracial Marriage and the Law in the Lower South, 1865–1900," *American Nineteenth Century History* 6, no. 1 (2005): 57–76.

16. See Bryan Wagner, "Charles Chesnutt and the Epistemology of Racial Violence," *American Literature* 73, no. 2 (2001): 311–37. "In November 1898 a corrupt election transformed the city of Wilmington, North Carolina. Ballot boxes were stuffed, and black voters were kept away from the polls by patrols of armed white men. As a result, the city's racially integrated government was replaced by a new white supremacist regime. Two days later, the city erupted in violence. Apparently unsatisfied with their overwhelming victory, a white mob stormed the offices of a local black-owned newspaper and set them on fire. After the newspaper building burned to the ground, organized patrols of armed white men took over the public spaces of the city. They stopped any African Americans they found, searched them for weapons, and ordered them off the streets. Although some tried to resist, they were massively outgunned by a white horde armed with 'nearly two thousand Winchester rifles' and a new rapid-fire machine gun mounted on a cart to patrol the 'negro quarters of the city.' As the violence intensified, many black families fled to the surrounding swamps, where they hid for several days before returning to a radically altered city many of them soon left for good" (311).

17. Charles Chesnutt to Walter Hines Page, November 11, 1898, in "*To Be an Author,*" 116.

18. Brook Thomas, "The Legal and Literary Complexities of U.S. Citizenship around 1900," *Law and Literature* 22, no. 2 (2010): 307–24; Bryan Wagner, "Charles Chesnutt and the Epistemology of Racial Violence," *American Literature* 73, no. 2 (2001): 311–37.

19. Matthew R. Martin, "The Two-Faced New South: The Plantation Tales of Thomas Nelson Page and Charles W. Chesnutt," *Southern Literary Journal* 30, no. 2 (Spring 1998): 18.

20. Gavin Jones, "Signifying Songs: The Double Meaning of Black Dialect in the Work of George Washington Cable," *American Literary History* 9, no. 2 (1997): 244–67.

21. Dale E. Peterson, *Up from Bondage: The Literatures of Russian and African American Soul* (Durham: Duke University Press, 2000), 95. Some literary scholars have remarked on the Dickensian naming of Chesnutt's characters, which often suggest their personality or status. For such remarks on *The House behind the Cedars* (1900), see Sylvia Lyons Render, *Charles W. Chesnutt* (Boston: Twayne, 1980); and Sally Ann H. Ferguson, "'Frank Fowler': A Chesnutt Racial Pun," *South Atlantic Review* 50, no. 2 (May 1985): 47–53.

22. Eric Lott, *Love and Theft: Blackface Minstrelsy and the American Working Class* (Oxford: Oxford University Press, 1995), 22; hereafter cited parenthetically.

23. At the end of one story in which a slave master is turned into a slave, to give an example, John condescendingly praises Uncle Julius for adding a moral at the end of his tale, saying that "[the moral] might have escaped us otherwise" (101). Yet we observe that the moral *did* indeed escape John, who refuses to see a connection between his own life and the appeal made for "w'ite folks" to be more understanding about "po'ign'ant niggers w'at ain'had no chanst ter l'arn" and be kinder to "po'people" (100). His wife, Annie, is moved by the story, however, to grant Uncle Julius's grandson a second chance to work in the household without consulting with him first. The story ends with John's dismay and inability to undo Annie's decision, to be relished: "I did

not wish the servants to think there was any conflict of authority in the household, I let the boy stay" (102).

24. For a very thorough analysis of this, see Nowatzki, "'Passing' in a White Genre," 25–29.

25. Chesnutt to Houghton, Mifflin, & Co., October 26, 1901, in *"To Be an Author,"* 161.

26. "John and Masa Tales," in Zora Neale Hurston, *Every Tongue Got to Confess: Negro Folk-Tales from the Gulf States* (New York: HarperCollins, 2001), 83–102.

27. William Andrews, *The Literary Career of Charles W. Chesnutt* (Baton Rouge: Louisiana State University Press, 1980).

28. Charles Chesnutt, *The Journals of Charles W. Chesnutt* (Durham: Duke University Press, 1994), 139. The entry date is May 29, 1880.

29. Robert M. Farnsworth, introduction to *The Conjure Woman*, viii.

30. Ben Slote, "Listening to 'the Goophered Grapevine' and Hearing Raisins Sing," *American Literary History* 6, no. 4 (1994): 684–94. Slote refers to a review from 1899 that sees Chesnutt's stories as "relief from serious fiction of the day," explaining that this happens only if one "does not recognize that the transformation of people into consumable, edible things describes—nearly literalizes—the dehumanizing economic logic of race oppression" (686).

31. Andrews, *The Literary Career of Charles W. Chesnutt*, 52. Robert C. Nowatzki notes the visual reference to Joel Chandler Harris's Uncle Remus stories in the cover of Chesnutt's *Conjure Woman*: "This resemblance [between Julius and Remus] was emphasized on the book's original cover, which featured a smiling balding old black man framed by two mischievous-looking white rabbits. Since there were no rabbits in *The Conjure Woman*, the publishers were clearly trying to capitalize on the success of Harris's Uncle Remus and his retellings of the Brer Rabbit stories" ("'Passing' in a White Genre," 23).

32. Howells, "A Psychological Counter-Current," *North American Review* 173, no. 541 (December 1901): 872–88. His enthusiastic support for Chesnutt's work waned after the publication of *The Marrow of Tradition* in 1905, about which he made the oft-quoted comment that Chesnutt's courage in writing the novel has "more justice than mercy in it" and that "the book is, in fact, bitter, bitter" (882).

33. Anne E. Boyd, "'What! Has She Got into the "Atlantic"?': Women Writers, the *Atlantic Monthly*, and the Formation of the American Canon," *American Studies* 39, no. 3 (Fall 1998): 5–36.

34. Chestnutt to Walter Hines Page, May 20, 1898, in *"To Be an Author,"* 105.

35. Ibid., 107.

36. R. D. Connor, "Walter Hines Page: A Southern Nationalist," *Journal of Social Forces* 2 (1924): 164.

37. Walter Hines Page, "The Rebuilding of Old Commonwealths," *Atlantic Monthly* 89 (May 1902): 659.

38. Burton J. Hendricks, *The Life and Letters of Walter H. Page*, vol. 1 (New York: Doubleday, Page, 1922), 48.

39. Rayburn S. Moore, "Walter Hines Page, Intersectional Ambassador," *Southern Literary Journal* 10 (1978): 166.

40. Walter Hines Page, *A Publisher's Confession* (New York: Doubleday, Page, 1905); hereafter cited parenthetically.

41. "We try to make friends for his book and for him throughout the reading world. We all take a personal interest in him and in his future. We invest our money, our good

will, our work, our experience, our advice, our enthusiasm in him and in his future" (166); "Not one of them has failed to recognize or to encourage a high literary purpose if it were sanely directed," he writes, and that "every one of them every year invests in books and authors that they know cannot yield a direct or immediate profit, and they make these investments because they feel ennobled by trying to do a service to literature" (75). In short, publishing is "the least profitable of professions, except preaching and teaching, to each of which it is a sort of cousin" (23).

42. As Young explains, Boni and Liveright advertised *Cane* (1923) as "a book about Negroes by a Negro," despite Jean Toomer's express request not to promote the book along such racial lines. Nella Larsen agreed to switch the title of her second novel from "Nig" to *Passing* (1929) because an editor at Knopf felt the original title "might be too inflammatory for a novel by an unproven writer, while 'Passing,' and the phenomenon's connection to miscegenation, would incite interest without giving offence" (Thadious M. Davis, *Nella Larsen: Novelist of the Harlem Renaissance: A Woman's Life Unveiled* [Baton Rouge: Louisiana State University, 1994], 306–7). Richard Wright revised and deleted several scenes in *Native Son* (1940) depicting Bigger Thomas masturbating, as well as those showing Mary Dalton's desire for Bigger, in order to publish his first novel as a Book of the Month Club main selection. Zora Neale Hurston criticized American racial policy in her autobiography, *Dust Tracks on a Road* (1942), noting that "President Roosevelt could extend his four freedoms to people right here in America." But she cut this passage and others like it after an editor at Lippincott wrote, "Suggest eliminating international opinions as irrelevant to autobiography" (Robert E. Hemenway, *Zora Neale Hurston: A Literary Biography* [Urbana: University of Illinois Press, 1977], 287–88). Toni Morrison revised the last "racially charged but figuratively coherent" word of *Beloved* (1987) at her editor's request ("Home" in *The House That Race Built*, ed. Wahneema Lubiano [New York: Vintage, 1998], 8), and changed the title of *Paradise* (1998) from "War" to allay Knopf's concerns (Alice Mulrine, "*Paradise* Follows *Beloved* and *Jazz*: Toni Morrison Talks about Her Latest Novel," *Princeton Alumni Weekly*, March 11, 1998, 22).

43. John K. Young in *Black Writers, White Publishers: Marketplace Politics in Twentieth-Century African American Literature* (Jackson: University of Mississippi Press, 2006), 4; hereafter cited parenthetically.

44. Historically, the amount of "head tax" imposed on the Chinese was ten dollars, as stipulated in the Act to Restrict and Regulate Chinese Immigration of 1885. This was raised to fifty dollars in 1896, one hundred dollars in 1900, and five hundred dollars in 1903.

45. "The presence of the Chinese affects the material and moral interests of the Canadian people, that the Chinese work cheap and therefore white men cannot compete with them, that they are gamblers and grossly immoral, that they introduce disease, cost the public much money and delay the development of the country."

46. *The Oxford English Dictionary* lists "boodle" as "*v.* (*trans.*) to bribe; *intr.*, to practice bribery."

47. Some attribute this designation to Frank Chin's introduction to Chinese and Japanese American literature in *Aiiieeeee!* (1974), but technically, he describes her as "an English-born Eurasian [who] wrote and published short fiction in the nineteenth century. She was one of the first to speak for an Asian American sensibility that was neither Asian nor white American" (xxi). References to Sui Sin Far as the first Asian American writer are ubiquitous; the following articles, among others, give extensive

focus: S. E. Solberg, "Sui Sin Far/Edith Eaton: The First Chinese-American Fictionist," *MELUS* 8, no. 1 (1981): 27–39; Xiao-Huang Yin, "Between the East and West: Sui Sin Far—the First Chinese-American Woman Writer," *Arizona Quarterly* 47, no. 4 (1991): 49–84; Yu Ning, "Fanny Fern and Sui Sin Far: The Beginning of an Asian American Voice," *Women and Language* 19, no. 2 (1996): 44–47; and Sau-ling Cynthia Wong, "Chinese American Literature," in *An Interethnic Companion to Asian American Literature*, ed. King-Kok Cheung (Cambridge: Cambridge University Press, 1997).

48. Annette White-Parks, *Sui Sin Far/ Edith Maude Eaton: A Literary Biography* (Urbana: University of Illinois Press, 1995), 101; hereafter cited parenthetically.

49. Sui Sin Far, "In the Land of the Free," *Independent*, September 2, 1909, 505.

50. Sui Sin Far, "Leaves from the Mental Portfolio of an Eurasian," *Independent*, January 21, 1909, 129; hereafter cited parenthetically.

51. Lorraine Dong and Marlon Hom, "Defiance or Perpetuation: An Analysis of Characters in *Mrs. Spring Fragrance*," in *Chinese America: History and Perspectives*, ed. Him Mark Lai, Ruthanne Lum McCunn, and Judy Young (San Francisco: Chinese Historical Society of America, 1987), 139–68.

52. Mike Davis, *City of Quartz: Excavating the Future in Los Angeles* (New York: Verso, 1990).

53. Dominika Ferens, "*Native Americans, Chinese, and White Progressivists in the Land of Sunshine*, 1895–1909," *American Transcendental Quarterly* 15, no. 4 (December 2001): 305–16.

54. William Hayes Ward, "Conflicts and Conquests," *Independent*, December 3, 1908.

55. In 1885, the *Independent* reported and criticized the Cleveland administration's suggestion of further anti-Chinese legislation:

> This whole anti-Chinese movement, whether in Congress or out of it, is the sheerest humbug imaginable. There is no occasion for it, except that which partisan politics and ignorance have made; and twenty-five years hence the American people will be ashamed of it.

It reported the modifications to the Chinese Exclusion Act as "A Mitigation of Abomination" (1/18/1883) and the Geary anti-Chinese Bill as a "Bold Bad Bill" (4/14/1892). In anticipation of the vote for the Geary Act, the missionary Rev. S. L. Baldwin wrote a short piece in which he condemned the Chinese Exclusion Act itself, saying, "we are disgracing ourselves before the civilized world by this iniquitous legislation. Surely, the time has come when the Christian people of the land should notify their representatives in Congress that they will not tolerate a single additional act of oppressive legislation against these people" ("Beauties of Our Anti-Chinese Legislation," 4/17/1890), and after the passage of the Geary Act, he explained that it was not simply a renewal of the same bill but "far surpassed in infamy" of the 1882:

This act first undertook to extend for ten years all the anti-Chinese legislation then in force. It then provided that all Chinese laborers in the country should within one year register themselves at the office of the Internal Revenue Collector, producing proof of their right to be in the country; and that all who failed to do so before the end of one year should be liable to imprisonment and deportation to China. All who registered were to have certificates which they should be ready at all times to produce as evidence of their right to be here.[I]t is an hour of utterly unnecessary, yet of deep and lasting disgrace. If, in the good providence of God, some way out is revealed, it will be better fortune than we deserve. (S. L. Baldwin, D.D., "The Crowning Infamy," May 11, 1893)

It also introduced *Zion's Herald*'s criticism of the Geary Act:

> It would be difficult to devise a bill more malignant in its provisions than the recently enacted Chinese Exclusion Act. It is a plain concession to the demands of the "sand-lot" agitators, and a burning disgrace to a Christian nation. (5/19/1892)

56. William Hayes Ward, "The Record of the Independent." *Independent*, November 7, 1912.

57. Sean McCann, "Connecting Links: The Anti-Progressivism of Sui Sin Far," *Yale Journal of Criticism* 12, no. 1 (1999): 73–88.

58. Ward, "Conflicts and Conquests."

59. Boies Penrose, "Chinese Exclusion and the Problems of Immigration," *Independent*, January 2, 1902.

60. Lee Chew, "The Biography of a Chinaman," trans. Joseph M. Singleton, *Independent*, February 19, 1903.

61. Hamilton Holt, "William Hayes Ward," *Independent*, September 11, 1916.

62. Jeffrey Sklansky, *The Soul's Economy: Market Society and Selfhood in American Thought, 1820–1920* (Chapel Hill: University of North Carolina Press, 2002), 76.

63. "Yellow Peril," *Independent*, March 3, 1904.

64. William Hayes Ward, "Forty-Five Years at the Editorial Desk," *Independent*, November 13, 1913.

2 / The Making of the Cosmopolitan Subject

Note: "BL Jessica Hagedorn Papers" indicates Jessica Tarahata Hagedorn Papers, BANC MSS 2007/160, Bancroft Library, University of California, Berkeley.

1. Jessica Hagedorn, *Danger and Beauty* (New York: Penguin, 1993), ix.

2. Ronald Takaki, *Strangers from Another Shore* (Boston: Little, Brown, 1989), 272.

3. James Sobredo, "From Manila Bay to Daly City: Filipinos in San Francisco," in *Reclaiming San Francisco: History, Politics, Culture*, ed. James Brook, Chris Carlsson, and Nancy J. Peters (San Francisco: City Lights, 2001), 274.

4. Shirley Geok-lin Lim, "Assaying the Gold: Or, Contesting the Ground of Asian American Literature," "Culture and Everyday Life" issue, *New Literary History* 24, no. 1 (Winter 1993): 147.

5. Ibid. In the Angel Island Poems, carved by the Chinese detainees held in the detention barracks between 1910 and 1940, a "utopianist vision of a future of plenty is reconfigured against the reality of discriminatory immigration policies, as the expansive dream of 'the Gold Mountain' is contracted to the figure of 'a prison on the mountain'" (148).

6. Frank Chin, "Introduction to Yardbird Reader #3," *Yardbird Reader* 3 (1974): vi.

7. See Estella Habal's *San Francisco's International Hotel: Mobilizing the Filipino American Community in the Anti-Eviction Movement* (Philadelphia: Temple University Press, 2007).

8. On the San Francisco Renaissance, see Michael Davidson, *The San Francisco Renaissance: Poetics and Community at Mid-Century* (New York: Cambridge University Press, 1989). Hagedorn herself gave credit to Rexroth, including an interview with Joyce Jenkins in *Poetry Flash* (BL Jessica Hagedorn Papers, 10:5), *San Francisco Examiner* (10:6), and *Seattle Post- Intelligencer* (8:13). The most detailed description of their meeting, in Hagedorn's words, is the following: "A family friend sent my poems

to Kenneth Rexroth, who at the time had a cultural column in a San Francisco paper. He asked to meet me, and he really became sort of a mentor to me. I was 16 at the time, and responsible for getting my first book published" (10:6, interview from *Dispatch*, the newsletter for the Center for American Culture Studies at Columbia University, Fall 1987).

9. As individual poems, Asian American poetry had already appeared throughout the century in literary journals, and Asian American writers (whom Chin et al. had not invited to submit to their anthology) had already published stand-alone collections of poems from smaller presses. Greg San Diego's *Soliloquies in a Philippine Garden* was published by a small theater press called Pisani Press in 1956; Jose Garcia also published two collections of poems in 1958 (Boston-based Wake Press) and 1959 (New Directions); Yasuo Sasaki followed with *Ascension* (1968) from Balconet Press.

10. Kenneth Rexroth, introduction to *Four Young Women: Poems* (New York: McGraw-Hill, 1973), x; hereafter cited parenthetically.

11. Kenneth Rexroth, *American Poetry in the Twentieth Century* (New York: Seabury Press, 1974), 137.

12. Ibid., 138.

13. Kobena Mercer, *Welcome to the Jungle* (New York: Routledge, 1994), 284.

14. For full discussions on this point, see Robert Stam, "Multiculturalism and the Neoconservatives," in *Dangerous Liaisons: Gender, Nation, and Postcolonial Perspectives*, ed. Anne McClintock, Aamir Mufti, and Ella Shohat (Minneapolis: Minnesota University Press, 1997), 188–203; John Brenkman, "Multiculturalism and Criticism," in *English Inside Out: The Places of Literary Criticism*, ed. Susan Gubar and Jonathan Kamholtz (New York: Routledge, 1993), 87–101.

15. Jessica Hagedorn maintained in response to my question (interview, July 27, 2012) that the character is fictional. However, many of her readers at the time recognized this as a satire of Kenneth Rexroth, as seen in Esther Sugai's review, in which she writes that "Silver Daddy, the opulent, Japan-crazy slumlord, is clearly Kenneth Rexroth" (*International Examiner*, April 1, 1982, in BL Jessica Hagedorn Papers, 1:21). Hagedorn herself wrote to Stephen Vincent that asking Kenneth Rexroth for a blurb of *Pet Food and Tropical Apparitions* was not a good idea for this reason ("definitely *not* Kenneth—I don't think he'd appreciate his caricature in the novel!") (March 21, 1981, BANC MSS 94/17, carton 1, folder 11).

16. Giorgio Agamben, *Homo Sacer: Sovereign Power and Bare Life, trans. Daniel Heller-Roazen* (Stanford: Stanford University Press, 1998), 170.

17. In the U.S. Northwest (Abbott), East Coast (Reed, Bambara), South (Al Young, Ernest Gaines), and Midwest (Toni Morrison); in Panama (Thomas), Nicaragua (Roberto Vargas), Puerto Rico (Victor Hernandez Cruz), and the Philippines (Hagedorn, Cyn Zarco).

18. Bruce Dick and Amritjit Singh, eds. *Conversations with Ishmael Reed* (Jackson: Mississippi University Press, 2009), 78.

19. Ishmael Reed, "Introduction, I," *Yardbird Reader* 1 (1972).

20. John K. Young, *Black Writers, White Publishers: Marketplace Politics in Twentieth-Century African American Literature* (Jackson: Mississippi University Press, 2010), 68.

21. Rexroth, introduction to *Four Young Women: Poems*, x.

22. "The Writer as Seer: Ishmael Reed on Ishmael Reed," in *Conversations with Ishmael Reed*, ed. Bruce Dick and Amritjit Singh (Jackson: University Press of Mississippi,

1995), 68. In this interview from *Black World* (June 1974), Reed narrates the following turn of events: "Roberta Palm of Howard University Press went to *Publishers Weekly* (3/4/1974) and told them, 'We didn't realize until we looked into it that Asian Americans hadn't been published before,' when she knew better and got the idea for publishing *Aiiieeeee!: An Introduction to Asian-American Writing* from *Yardbird Reader: I and II.* In Volume II we printed, in 1973, an introduction from the very anthology they say they found first. In fact, she called Shawn Wong and asked him the identity of Asian-American writers in *Yardbird.* They don't give us an acknowledgment at all in their edition. Isn't that *gauche*?"

23. Chin acknowledges a significant amount of tension that had historically existed between African Americans and Asian Americans. As when Chin declares that the *Yardbird Reader* is "no inter-racial treaty, vision of Utopia or crazy avant garde stunt," conflict is only overwhelmed by the mutual suspicion of white cultural traditions. Chin takes time to dispel the notion that writing is innately "an exclusively white practice," expressing the editors' collective disinterest in following what had been a predominantly white literary tradition. The volume is thus dedicated to John Okada, Louis Chu, Duke Ellington, and William Gardner Smith, expressing the lasting impact of Chu's passing in 1970 and the large sense of loss felt in the passing of Okada, Ellington, and Smith in 1974.

24. For an analysis of this volume that discusses the role of Yardbird Publishing and Barbara Smith's Kitchen Table Press in shaping Afro-Asian collaborations, see Cheryl Higashida's essay "Not Just a 'Special Issue': Gender, Sexuality and Post-1965 Afro Asian Coalition Building in the *Yardbird Reader* and *This Bridge Called My Back*," in *Afro Asia: Revolutionary Political and Cultural Connections between African Americans and Asian American*, ed. Fred Ho and Bill V. Mullen (Durham: Duke University Press, 2008), 220–55.

25. Back matter, Jessica Hagedorn, *Dangerous Music* (San Francisco: Momo's Press, 1975).

26. Thulani Nkabinde, "Review of *Dangerous Music* by Jessica Tarahata Hagedorn," *Yardbird Reader* 5 (1976): 31–33.

27. Ibid.

28. Irene Reti and Randall Jarrell, eds., *Alta and the History of Shameless Hussy Press, 1969–1989* (Santa Cruz: University of California, Santa Cruz, University Library, 2001). Used with permission from the Regional History Project, UCSC Library Special Collections and Archives Department.

29. Gloria Anzaldúa, *Borderlands: The New Mestiza = La Frontera* (San Francisco: Aunt Lute Books, 1999).

30. Initially set up in Baltimore, Diana Press moved to Oakland in 1977 to join the Women's Press Collective, but the vandalism made it impossible to continue, and it had to establish itself exclusively as a print shop thereafter: "Paint, ink, and cleanser were poured into the presses, negatives and cover plates were ruined and typesetting was ripped up page by page. With both backlist and forthcoming books destroyed, including 5,000 copies of Rita Mae Brown's *A Plain Brown Rapper*, the press closed down its publishing program" (Cathy N. Davidson, Linda Wagner-Martin, and Elizabeth Ammons, eds., *Oxford Companion to Women's Writing in the U.S.* [Cambridge: Oxford University Press, 1995], 704).

31. Alta's account in an interview by Irene Reti as a part of the UC Santa Cruz Regional History Project continues: "It wasn't the rednecks in the suburbs doing it. One of the theories was FBI agitators. But we have no way of knowing. Evidence came

out two or two and a half years later that it was all women who destroyed Diana Press. It was women threatening us" (Reti and Jarrell, eds. *Alta and the History of Shameless Hussy Press, 1969–1989*, 18–19).

32. "Biographical Notes," in *Four Young Women: Poems*, 147: "An editor of the forthcoming anthology of literature and graphics, *Third World Women*, to be published by the Third World Communications Collective, she is presently working on a one-act play, *Chiquita Banana*, evoking Carmen Miranda, to be included in the anthology."

33. Karin Ikas, *Chicana Ways: Conversations with Ten Chicana Writers* (Reno: University of Nevada Press, 2001), 5.

34. Jessica Hagedorn, introduction to *Charlie Chan Is Dead: An Anthology of Contemporary Asian American Fiction*, ed. Hagedorn (New York: Penguin, 1993), xxiv.

35. Ibid.

36. Jessica Hagedorn Papers, BANC MSS 2007/160, carton 9.

37. Ngugi wa Thiong'o, *Decolonising the Mind: The Politics of Language in African Literature* (London: James Currey, 1981).

38. Jessica Hagedorn Papers, BANC MSS 2007/160, carton 9. The quote is from Rushdie's *Imaginary Homelands: Essays and Criticism 1981–1991* (New York: Viking, 1991), 66.

39. Paule Marshall, "From the Poets in the Kitchen," *Callalloo* 18 (Spring-Summer 1983): 22–30; Tejumola Olanyan, *Scars of Conquest/ Resistance: Masks of the Invention of Cultural Identities in African, African-American, and Caribbean Drama* (New York: Oxford University Press, 1995).

40. Jessica Hagedorn, interview by author, August 10, 2012.

41. Hagedorn to Maxine Hong Kingston. Maxine Hong Kingston Papers 1952–1999, BANC MSS 85/20 c, box 24, folder "Hagedorn, Jessica Tarahata, 1949–1981–92."

42. Han Ong to Jessica Hagedorn, December 7, 1993, Jessica Hagedorn Papers, BANC MSS 2007/160, carton 11:21.

43. *San Francisco Sunday Examiner*, February 10, 1974, Jessica Hagedorn Papers, BANC MSS 2007/160, carton 10.

44. For a useful account of this performative aspect within a genealogy of San Francisco poets, see "Poetry Readings/ Reading Poetry: San Francisco Bay Area, 1958–1980," in *The Poetry Reading: A Contemporary Compendium on Language and Performance*, ed. Stephen Vincent and Ellen Zweig (San Francisco: Momo's Press, 1981), which will be cited later in the chapter.

45. Christine Bacareza Balance, "Dancing to Rock & Roll Poetry," *BOOM: A Journal of California Studies* 3, no. 2 (Summer 2013): 72–81.

46. Jessica Hagedorn, "Makebelieve Music," in *The Poetry Reading*, ed. Vincent and Zweig, 139.

47. Jessica Hagedorn, "Pet Food," in *Pet Food and Tropical Apparitions* (1981; rpt. in *Hagedorn, Danger and Beauty* [New York: Penguin, 1993], 79–170), 85; hereafter cited parenthetically.

48. Suzanne E. Smith, *Dancing in the Street: Motown and the Cultural Politics of Detroit* (Cambridge: Harvard University Press, 2000).

49. Richard Dyer, *Stars* (London: British Film Institute, 1979), 153. I do also have in mind Dyer's analyses in essays included in *Only Entertainment* (London: Routledge, 1992).

50. Tom Engelhardt, *The End of Victory Culture: Cold War America and the Disillusioning of a Generation* (New York: Basic, 1995), 138. Engelhardt continues: "In 1955, twenty of the top twenty-five records were by blacks; by 1958 only four of the top twenty-five represented black styles." Leerom Medovoi also points out in "Mapping the Rebel Image: Postmodernism and the Masculinist Politics of Rock in the U.S.A." (*Cultural Critique* 20 [Winter 1991–92]: 153–88) the following: "Given the profound threat that a liaison between a white woman and a black man posed to the symbolic order," Medovoi has noted, "the mass media (especially visual media) censored and resisted this first wave of black rockers'—Fats Domino, Little Richard, etc.—construction of their public rebel images for white audiences" (165).

51. Michael Bertrand, *Race, Rock, and Elvis* (Urbana: University of Illinois Press, 2000).

52. Greil Marcus, "Elvis Again," *Threepenny Review*, no. 92 (Winter 2003): 26.

53. Dyer, *Stars*, 60. Dyer names Sheila Whitaker's grouping of Marlon Brando and James Dean together as the "rebel hero" type, alongside John Garfield, Montgomery Clift, Albert Finney, Paul Newman, and Steve McQueen (Sheila Whitaker, "The Rebel Hero," *Hollywood and the Great Stars Monthly*, no. 8 [1975]: 10–13).

54. Peter Biskind, "Rebel without a Cause: Nicholas Ray in the Fifties," *Film Quarterly* 28, no. 1 (Autumn 1974): 32–38.

55. Fredric Jameson, "Reification and Utopia and Mass Culture," *Social Text*, no. 1 (Winter 1979): 130–48.

56. Alice Walker, "Nineteen Fifty-Five," in *You Can't Keep a Good Woman Down: Stories* (New York: Harcourt, Brace, and Jovanovich, 1981), 9, 7.

57. Marla Johnson, "You *Just* Can't Keep a Good Woman Down': Alice Walker Sings the Blues," *African American Review* 30, no. 2 (Summer 1996): 221–36. As Johnson puts it, "throughout Presley's career, his success was largely due to his numerous 'covers' of R&B records by African American composers and performers. While Presley made an enormous amount of money singing and recording the songs of African Americans, the African American originators saw very little. This longstanding 'tradition' of racism and exploitation in the American music industry, which appeared in a slightly different guise in the classic blues era, dates back to minstrelsy" (231).

58. Medovoi, "Mapping the Rebel Image," 164. Medovoi offers a convincing reading that calls our attention to the complex way in which Little Richard's "Good Golly, Miss Molly" or Bill Haley's "Rock around the Clock" "(cinematically embedded in a narrative of juvenile delinquency) positioned its subject to identify with and join the black male in his alleged threat to domestic white womanhood, symbol of the despised (white) social order," and goes on to argue that "the racial narrative reversal articulated by fifties rock was accomplished by the 'crossover' of a white teenage audience" (165); "Rock 'n' roll was not articulated by some change in the African-American musical tradition of rhythm and blues, nor simply by white musicians' 'appropriation' of it" (165).

59. bell hooks, "Eating the Other: Desire and Resistance," in *Race and Representation*, by hooks, 21–39 (Boston: South End Press, 1992). Hooks refers to Steve Perry's essay "The Politics of Crossover," but I also think this point should be maintained as a critical counterpoint to the discussion of any "crossover" figure, such as Phillip Brian Harper's study "Synethesia, 'Crossover,' and Blacks in Popular Music," *Social Text* 23 (Autumn–Winter 1989): 102–21.

60. Arjun Appadurai, *Modernity at Large: Cultural Dimensions of Globalization* (Minneapolis: University of Minnesota Press, 1994), 29.

61. Hagedorn, introduction to *Charlie Chan Is Dead*, xxii.

62. See Greg B. Felker, "Southeast Asian Industrialisation and the Changing Global Production System," in "Governing the Asia Pacific: Beyond the 'New Regionalism,'" special issue, *Third World Quarterly* 24, no. 2 (April 2003): 255–82.

63. Daniel Bivons, "Alice the Child-Imperialist and the Games of Wonderland," *Nineteenth Century Literature* 41, no. 2 (1986): 143–71. Bivons casts Alice as the "imperialist child" who continually fails to understand the logic and rules in an incommensurable system that governs Wonderland; a range of Alice's actions can be read as "imperialistic," like moments of bullying, tendencies to produce her own self-justifying evidence, and the continual efforts to "know."

64. The letter is dated November 18, 1821 (George Sand, *Correspondance* 1, ed. George Lubin [Paris: Editions Garnier Frères, 1964–71]); René Doumic's translation of this sentence in the same letter is "I know my way about" (*George Sand: Some Aspects of Her Life and Writings* [London: Chapman and Hall, 1910], 24).

65. Slavoj Zizek, "Multiculturalism, Or, the Cultural Logic of Multinational Capitalism," *New Left Review* 225 (1997): 28–51.

66. Marge Piercy, *Braided Lives* (1982; rpt., New York: Crest Fawcett, 1986), 21; hereafter cited parenthetically.

67. In Baudelaire's words, "inferior to Sade." Walter Benjamin, *Arcades Project* (Cambridge: Belknap Press of Harvard University Press, 1999), 277.

68. See Rita Felski, *The Gender of Modernity* (Cambridge: Harvard University Press, 1995).

69. See George Sand, *A Woman's Version of the Faust Legend: The Seven Strings of the Lyre*, trans. George A. Kennedy (Chapel Hill: University of North Carolina Press, 1989), 7; hereafter cited parenthetically.

70. Doris Kadish, "George Sand, Napoleon, and Slavery," *George Sand et l'empire des lettres*, ed. Anne E. McCall-Saint-Saëns (New Orleans: Presses Universitaires du Nouveau Monde, 2004), 3–24.

71. Alex Woloch, *The One vs. the Many: Minor Characters and the Space of the Protagonist in the Novel* (Princeton: Princeton University Press, 2003), 7.

72. In a deleted section from the first draft of "Pet Food," George explains: "He got his nickname 'boogie' because he was the best dancer in high school. Even the black kids gave him that!" (Momo's Press Papers, BANC MS 690/41, carton 1:4, p. 69 of "editor's copy").

73. Susan Evangelista, "Jessica Hagedorn and Manila Magic," *MELUS* 18, no. 4 (1993): 41–52.

74. For U.S. imperialism in the Philippines in the early decades of twentieth century, see Vincente L. Rafael, "White Love: Surveillance and Nationalist Resistance in the U.S. Colonization of the Philippines," in *Cultures of United States Imperialism*, ed. Amy Kaplan and Donald E. Pease (Durham: Duke University Press, 1993), 185–218.

75. Noam Chomsky, *For Reasons of State* (New York: Pantheon, 1973), 47.

76. Sandra Gilbert and Susan Gubar, *The Madwoman in the Attic: The Woman Writer and the Nineteenth-Century Literary Imagination* (1973; New Haven: Yale University Press, 2000).

77. Gayatri Chakravorty Spivak, "Three Women's Texts and a Critique of Imperialism," *Critical Inquiry* 12 (Autumn 1985): 243–61.

78. Carol Tinker to Jessica Hagedorn, July 27/1971, Jessica Hagedorn Papers, BANC MSS 2007/160 carton 11:24.

79. Carol Tinker to Jessica Hagedorn, April 17, 1972, Jessica Hagedorn Papers, BANC MSS 2007/160 carton 11:24.

80. Stephen Vincent to Jessica Hagedorn, December 8, 1979, Momo's Press Records, 1972–1986 BANC MSS 97/41.

81. Hagedorn, *Danger and Beauty*, x.

82. Francis Raven, "A Walk with Stephen Vincent," *Rain Taxi: A Review of Books*, Summer 2007, online edition, www.raintaxi.com/a-walk-with-stephen-vincent/.

83. Ruth Abbott and Ira Simmons, "An Interview with Ishmael Reed," in *Conversations with Ishmael Reed*, ed. Bruce Dick and Amritjit Singh (Jackson: University Press of Mississippi, 1995), 77; hereafter cited parenthetically.

84. Tom Beckett, "Interview with Stephen Vincent." August 30, 2007, E-X-C-H-A-N-G-E-V-A-L-U-E-S. http://willtoexchange.blogspot.com/2007/08/interview-with-stephen-vincent.html.

85. Vincent, *The Poetry Reading*, 48.

86. Stephen Vincent to Rei Magosaki, May 19, 2013.

87. Stephen Vincent, "Collecting in Ogoja" in Vincent, *The Poetry Reading*, 107.

88. Hagedorn has described herself in the following way: "My paternal grandfather came from Spain via Singapore to Manila. On my mother's side it's more mixture, with a Filipino mother and a father who was Scotch-Irish-French; you know, white American hybrid. And I also have on my father's side a great-great-grandmother who was Chinese" (Kay Bonetti, Greg Michalson, Speer Morgan, Jo Sapp, and Sam Stowers, eds., *Conversations with American Novelists: The Best Interviews from the "Missouri Review"* [Columbia: University of Missouri Press, 1997]), 219).

89. Stephen Vincent to Günter Ohnemus, February 24, 1982, Momo's Press Records, BANC MS 690/41, carton 1:11.

90. Stephen Vincent to Jessica Hagedorn, April 3, 1979, Momo's Press Records, BANC MSS 97/41, carton 1:11.

91. Jessica Hagedorn to Stephen Vincent, September 13, 1979, Momo's Press Records, BANC MSS 97/41, carton 1.

92. Stephen Vincent to Jessica Hagedorn, September 21, 1980, Momo's Press Records, BANC MSS 97/41, carton 1.

93. Stephen Vincent to Jessica Hagedorn, November 7, 1980, Momo's Press Records, BANC MSS 97/41, carton 1.

94. Helena Franklin to Jessica Hagedorn, February 1, 1989, Jessica Hagedorn Papers, BANC MSS 2007/160, 11:34, "Misc. Contracts."

95. Stephen Vincent to Rei Magosaki, November 2, 2013.

3 / L.A.–Paris–New York: The Parameters of Literary Production at the Turn of the Twenty-First Century

1. Ben Bandikian, *The Media Monopoly* (Boston: Beacon, 1983).

2. André Schiffrin, *The Business of Books: How the International Conglomerates Took over Publishing and Changed the Way We Read* (New York: Verso, 2001), 153; hereafter cited parenthetically.

3. Pantheon's authors also included the scientists François Jacob and Octave Mannoni; the social scientists Edgar Morin, Georges Banandier, and Jean Duvigneau; journalists including Claude Julien and André Fontaine, the editors of *Le Monde*; and historians such as Georges Duveaux, Georges Duby, and Moshe Lewin.

4. "The Media Business; Chief of Pantheon Is Said to Have Been Asked to Quit," *New York Times*, February 27, 1990; Edwin McDowell, "The Media Business; 4 Senior Editors Resign in Protest at Pantheon," *New York Times*, March 9, 1990; "More Pantheon Editors Resign in Protest," *New York Times*, May 3, 1990.

5. Scott Esposito, "How to Publish in a Recession: Coffee House Press's Allan Kornblum." *Conversational Reading*, February 17, 2009, http://conversationalreading.com/how-to-publish-in-a-recession-coffee-house-presss-allan-kornblum/.

6. Marianne Combs, "Minnesota: Land of Long-Lasting Small Presses," Minnesota Public Radio, October 8, 2004, http://news.minnesota.publicradio.org/features/2004/10/08_combsm_smallpresses/.

7. Coffee House mission statement, 2006.

8. Allan Kornblum, "Forum: Generations of Asian American Writers," *Asian American Literary Review*, May 10, 2012, http://aalr.binghamton.edu/0103forum/.

9. Shanon Gibney, "Double Vision, Three Times," *MN Artists.org*, May 7, 2007.

10. Kirby Olsen, *Andrei Codrescu and the Myth of America* (Jefferson, NC: McFarland, 2005), 176.

11. Terence Diggory, *Encyclopedia of the New York School Poets* (New York: Facts on File, 2009), 246.

12. William A. Katz, *The Columbia Granger's Guide to Poetry Anthologies* (New York: Columbia University Press, 1994), 26.

13. Coffee House Press mission statement; Esposito, "How to Publish in a Recession."

14. Anis Shivani, "Coffee House Press Editors and Writers on Indie Literary Publishing," *Huffington Post*, February 15, 2011, www.huffingtonpost.com/anis-shivani/coffee-house-press_b_819706.html; hereafter cited parenthetically as "Coffee House Press Editors."

15. King-Kok Cheung, ed., *Words Matter: Conversations with Asian American Writers* (Honolulu: University of Hawai'i Press, 2000), 323.

16. Ibid., 340; Terry Hong, "An Interview with Karen Tei Yamashita," *Book Slut*, July 2010, www.bookslut.com/features/2010_07_016303.php.

17. Karen Tei Yamashita, *Tropic of Orange* (Minneapolis: Coffee House Press, 1997), 81; hereafter cited parenthetically.

18. Scott Esposito, "How to Publish in a Recession: Coffee House Press's Allan Kornblum," February 17, 2009, *Scott Esposito's Blog*, http://conversationalreading.com/how-to-publish-in-a-recession-coffee-house-presss-allan-kornblum/.

19. "Vivendi Will Acquire Houghton Mifflin for .7 Billion," *New York Times*, June 2, 2001; for a discussion of Vivendi's role in privatization of water, see Maude Barlowe, *Blue Gold: The Fight to Stop the Corporate Theft of the World's Water* (New York: New Press, 2005), 101–28.

20. Harold T. Miller, *Publishing: A Leap from Mind to Mind* (Golden, CO: Fulcrum, 2003), xiii; hereafter cited parenthetically.

21. Jofie Ferrari-Adler, "Agents & Editors: A Q&A with Editor Janet Silver," *Poets & Writers*, July/August 2008, www.pw.org/content/agents_amp_editors_qampa_editor_janet_silver.

22. Ibid.

23. *Critical Inquiry* 8, no. 2 (Winter 1981): 178.

24. Katherine Roth, "Short Stories See a Rebirth," *Charleston Gazette*, April 23, 2000; Amber Qureshi, an editor at Picador USA, quoted by Quinn Dalton in "Paperback Originals: How Format Affects Reviewers and Sales," *Poets & Writers*, September/ October 2005, pw.org/content/paperback_originals_how_format_affects_reviews_and_sales.

25. Judith Rosen, "HM Trade and Reference Division 'On Target,'" *Publishers Weekly*, February 28, 2000; Roth, "Short Stories See a Rebirth."

26. Monique Truong, interview by Rei Magosaki, July 26, 2013, Brooklyn, New York.

27. Karen Ho, *Liquidated: An Ethnography of Wall Street* (Durham: Duke University Press, 2009), 5; hereafter cited parenthetically.

28. David J. Ravenscraft and F. M. Scherer, *Mergers, Sell-Offs, and Economic Efficiency* (Washington, DC: Brookings Institution, 1987).

29. Emily Witt, "Book Smart: Publisher of 'The Help' and Her Eye for Bestsellers," *New York Observer*, January 16, 2012, http://observer.com/2012/01/book-smart-publisher-of-the-help-and-her-eye-for-bestsellers/.

30. Pamela Hammonds, "Amy Einhorn Stops in for a Chat," *What Women Write*, January 25, 2010, http://whatwomenwritetx.blogspot.com/2010/01/amy-einhorn-stops-in-for-chat.html.

31. Min Jin Lee to Rei Magosaki, e-mail, July 25, 2014.

32. Gayle Weiswasser, "Q & A with Min Jin Lee, Author of *Free Food for Millionaires*," *Everyday I Write the Book*, November 27, 2007, http://everydayiwritethebookblog.com/2007/11/interview-with/ .

33. Janice Radway, *Reading the Romance: Women, Patriarchy, and Popular Literature* (Chapel Hill: University of North Carolina Press, 1991), 41–42.

34. Michael Szczerban, "Agents & Editors: Amy Einhorn," *Poets & Writers*, March/April 2014, www.pw.org/content/agents_editors_amy_einhorn.

35. "With more than 10 million copies sold, the #1 *New York Times* bestseller is now available in a special gift edition" (www.penguin.com/static/packages/us/the-help/index.php).

36. Sarah Lyall, "Book Notes; One Picasso, Two Writers and an Editor on the Spot," *New York Times*, July 7, 1993.

37. Szczerban, "Agents & Editors: Amy Einhorn."

38. In Asian American studies, the mainstream success of a given text as measured by mass popularity of the best seller traditionally led to stigmatization. Throughout the 1990s, best-selling Asian American writers met with hostility or boycotting in academic settings. However, this was not so much an ideological conflict between high art and commodified mass culture as it was over the issue of authenticity represented by the famous debate between Frank Chin and Maxine Hong Kingston in the early 1990s, narrated here by Garrett Hongo:

> [James Houston] told me that various articles had come out in the *Los Angeles Times*, *San Jose Mercury News*, and *San Francisco Chronicle* putting forward the story that there was a gender split between Asian American male writers and Asian American female writers. They put Frank Chin at the center of the argument, along with Maxine Hong Kingston and Amy Tan. They quoted Chin as saying that Kingston and Tan had won wide audience appeal because they pandered to white tastes and promulgated a stereotypical exotic image, particularly of Asian women. Chin used words like "traitors," "feminist assimilators," and "whores" when talking about Kingston and Tan, describing their work as "white racist art," then raging on about how Kingston, in particular, gets Chinese myth, language, and culture completely wrong. (*Under Western Eyes: Personal Essays from Asian America* [New York: Anchor, 1995], 18–19)

As long as the Asian American writers were claiming their rightful place in the cultural landscape of the United States as *American* writers, there is by default a break between the Asian country of the writer's family origin and the Asian American writers; even the most vocal among the "authentic" camp is an Asian American writer. There can only be varying degrees of proximity or familiarity with the "authentic" cultural source in Asia itself. Chin's claim, then, might be recast more simply as an assertion that best-selling works can be compromised, because only narratives that accommodate the desires of a white audience to consume familiar racist stereotypes of Asian Americans would be marketable to a mass audience. Chin himself may disagree, as he has written to Allan Kornblum of Coffee House Press as recently as spring of 2014 that "all the Yellows whites like to read trash Chinese and exalt Whites. That's what Whites like to read." Frank Chin, "Frank Chin's Letter to Allan Kornblum. Kornblum Responds," *[ChinTalks]*, April 22, 2014, http://chintalks.blogspot.com/2014_04_01_archive.html.

39. Christopher A. Shinn, "Homicidal Tendencies: Violence and the Global Economy in Asian American Pulp Fiction," in *Alien Encounters: Popular Culture in Asian America*, ed. Mimi Thi Nguyen and Thuy Linh Nguyen Tu (Durham: Duke University Press, 2007), 111.

40. Ibid., 113.

41. Pamela Thoma, *Asian American Women's Popular Literature: Feminizing Genres and Neoliberal Belonging* (Philadelphia: Temple University Press, 2014), 81.

42. See Charles Grisst, *Collateral Damaged: The Marketing of Consumer Debt to America* (New York: Bloomberg Press, 2009), 33.

43. Saskia Sassen, "The Logic of Finance: Abuse of Power and Systemic Crisis," in *How They Got Away with It: White Collar Criminals and the Financial Meltdown*, ed. Susan Will, Stephen Handelman, and David C. Brotherton (New York: Columbia University Press, 2013), 34.

44. Paige Crutcher, "Four Questions forAmy Einhorn," *Publisher's Weekly*, August 20, 2014, www.publishersweekly.com/pw/by-topic/industry-news/publisher-news/article/63717-four-questions-for-amy-einhorn.html.

45. Mike Davis, *City of Quartz: Excavating the Future in Los Angeles* (New York: Verso, 1990), 18.

46. Gloria Anzaldúa, *Borderlands/ La Frontera: The New Mestiza* (1987; San Francisco: Aunt Lute Books, 1999), cited more recently in Shelley Fisher Fishkin's call for locating the "transnational" as a central notion in American studies ("Crossroads of Cultures: The Transnational Turn in American Studies—Presidential Address for the American Studies Association, November 12, 2004," *American Quarterly* 57, no. 1 [2005]: 17–57).

47. Arjun Appadurai, *Modernity at Large* (Minneapolis: University of Minnesota Press, 1996), 169.

48. Tania Voon and Andrew D. Mitchell, "Time to Quit? Assessing International Investment Claims against Plain Tobacco Packaging in Australia," *Journal of International Economic Law* 14, no. 3 (2011): 515–52; Andrew D. Mitchell and Sebastian M. Wurtzberger, "Boxed In? Australia's Plain Tobacco Packaging Initiative and International Investment Law," *Arbitration International* 27 (2011): 623–52; Mark Davidson, "Big Tobacco vs Australia: Philip Morris Scores an Own Goal," *Conversation*, January 19, 2012, http://theconversation.com/big-tobacco-vs-australia-philip-morris-scores-an-own-goal-4967.

For corporate abuse of the investor-state dispute clause of free trade agreements, see Joseph E. Stiglitz, "Multinational Corporations: Balancing Rights and Responsibilities," *American Society of International Law Proceedings of the Annual Meeting* 101 (March 28–31, 2007): 3–60. See also Karsten Nowrot, "Transnational Corporations as Steering Subjects in International Economic Law: Two Competing Visions of the Future?," *Indiana Journal of Global Legal Studies* 18, no. 2 (Summer 2011): 803–42; and Peter Muchlinski, "The Changing Face of Transnational Business Governance: Private Corporate Law Liability and Accountability of Transnational Groups in a Post–Financial Crisis World," *Indiana Journal of Global Legal Studies* 18, no. 2 (Summer 2011): 665–705.

49. Mike Davis explains in *City of Quartz* that the Westside power structure in L.A., which "arose out of Jewish interests in entertainment, savings-and-loan, and suburban real-estate sectors," has been a major driving force that has fueled the power play between the "Downtown elite" led by "the Chandler dynasty of the *Times*" (71), and more recently supplanted by offshore capital.

50. Nancy Scheper-Hughes, "The Ends of the Body: Commodity Fetishism and the Global Traffic in Organs," *SAIS Review* 22, no. 1 (2002): 61–80.

51. Gilles Deleuze and Félix Guattari, "The Desiring-Machines," in *Anti-Oedipus: Capitalism and Schizophrenia,* trans. Robert Hurley, Seem Mark, and Helen R. Lane (1977; Minneapolis: University of Minnesota Press, 1983), 1.

52. Monique Truong, *The Book of Salt* (2003; Boston: Mariner, 2004), 107; hereafter cited parenthetically.

53. Gayatri Spivak, *In Other Worlds: Essays in Cultural Politics* (New York: Routledge, 1988), 205.

54. Wai Chee Dimock, *Through Other Continents: American Literature across Deep Time* (Princeton: Princeton University Press, 2008), 3.

55. Julia Kristeva, *The Power of Horror: An Essay on Abjection* (New York: Columbia University Press, 1982), 2; hereafter cited parenthetically.

56. Sigmund Freud, *The Uncanny,* trans. David McClintock (London: Penguin Classics, 2003), 124.

57. David Eng, "The End(s) of Race" *PMLA* 123, no. 5 (October 2008): 1479–93.

58. James Baldwin, "Mass Culture and the Creative Artist," *Daedalus* 89, no. 2 (Spring 1960): 376.

59. Min Jin Lee, *Free Food for Millionaires* (New York: Warner, 2007), 121; hereafter cited parenthetically.

60. Edith Wharton, *The House of Mirth* (1905; rpt., New York: Norton, 1990), 221.

61. See Maureen Montgomery, *Displaying Women: Spectacles of Leisure in Edith Wharton's New York* (New York: Routledge, 1998).

62. Edith Wharton, "The Vice of Reading," *North American Review* 177, no. 563 (October 1903): 514. As R. W. B. Lewis's introduction to *House of Mirth* (New York: Bantam Classics, 1984) recorded about its success, *The House of Mirth* sold 30,000 copies within ten days of its publication that swelled into 100,000 copies in a little over a month, which her editor, William Cary Brownell, called "the most rapid sales of any book ever published by Scribner."

63. Amy L. Blair, "Misreading *The House of Mirth,*" *Detroit Post*, November 17, 1906, qtd. in Shari Benstock, *No Gifts from Chance: A Biography of Edith Wharton* (New York: Penguin, 1995), 155.

64. John Cawelti, *Adventure, Mystery, and Romance: Formula Stories as Art and Popular Culture* (Chicago: University of Chicago Press, 1976), 19.

65. See Jessica Lyn Van Slooten, "Fashionably Indebted: Conspicuous Consumption, Fashion, and Romance in Sophie Kinsella's Shopaholic Trilogy," in *Chick Lit: The New Woman's Fiction*, ed, Suzanne Ferriss and Mallory Young (New York: Routledge, 2006): 219–38.

66. Thoma, *Asian American Women's Popular Literature*, 95.

67. Ibid., 80.

68. Albert C. Stevens, "Analysis of the Phenomena of the Panic in the United States in 1893," *Quarterly Journal of Economics* 8, no. 2 (January 1894): 117–48.

69. John F. Tinsley, "Depressions Past and Present," *Bulletin of the Business Historical Society*, 7, no. 2 (March 1933): 2–13.

70. Paul J. Miranti Jr., "The Mind's Eye of Reform: The ICC's Bureau of Statistics and Accounts and a Vision of Regulation, 1887–1940," *Business History Review* 63, no. 3 (Autumn 1989): 469–509. See also Herbert Hovenkamp, "Regulatory Conflict in the Gilded Age: Federalism and the Railroad Problem," *Yale Law Journal* 97, no. 6 (May 1988): 1017–72.

71. For some disputes over the actual effectiveness of government regulation, see Thomas LeDuc, "Carriers, Courts, and the Commodities Clause," special "Transportation" issue, *Business History Review* 39, no. 1 (Spring 1965): 57–73; and Charles L. Wright, "Issues in Freight Transportation Regulation: Comment," *American Journal of Agricultural Economics* 65, no. 1 (February 1983): 162–66.

72. Edward E. Cassady, "Muckraking in the Gilded Age," *American Literature* 13 (May 1941): 134–41.

73. Steward Denison, *An Iron Crown: A Tale of the Great Republic* (Chicago: Denison, 1885), 139.

74. Thoma, *Asian American Women's Popular Literature*, 92.

75. Walter Benjamin, *Illuminations*, trans. Harry Zohn (New York: Schocken, 1968), 60.

Index